HUMAN RIGHTS

A Reference Handbook

HUMAN RIGHTS

A Reference Handbook

Lucille Whalen
Immaculate Heart College Center

Introduction by David Hinkley

CONTEMPORARY WORLD ISSUES

ABC-CLIO

Santa Barbara, California
Oxford, England

Library of Congress Cataloging-in-Publication Data

Whalen, Lucille.
    Human rights : a reference handbook / Lucille Whalen ; introduction by David Hinkley.
      p. cm. — (Contemporary world issues)
    Includes bibliographies and indexes.
    Summary: A handbook listing books, periodicals, directories, non-print materials, and other information sources on human rights, intended for researchers, students, and activists.
    1. Human rights. [1. Human rights—Bibliography.] I. Title. II. Series.
    K3240.4.W46   1989   016.342′085—dc20   [016.342.285]
    89–15039

ISBN 0–87436–093–5 (alk. paper)
96 95 94 93 92 91 90   10 9 8 7 6 5 4 3 2

ABC-CLIO, Inc.
130 Cremona Drive, P.O. Box 1911
Santa Barbara, California 93116-1911

Clio Press Ltd.
55 St. Thomas' Street
Oxford, OX1 1JG, England

This book is Smyth-sewn and printed on acid-free paper ∞ .
Manufactured in the United States of America

Contents

Preface

FEW WILL ARGUE with the fact that human rights has become an increasingly important issue in today's world. Popular magazines have turned their attention to it; rock concerts have been given in its behalf; and many people, not only in the United States but around the world, are devoting considerable time and effort to its advocacy. The fortieth anniversary of the signing of the Universal Declaration of Human Rights, celebrated in 1988, heightened the awareness, among peoples everywhere, of the importance of dealing with human rights problems. As an abstract concept, everyone is *for* human rights, but when it comes to the concrete— which rights, for whom, under what circumstances—there are often differences of opinion.

This is perhaps the reason many writers do not define human rights except to say that they are the rights delineated in the Universal Declaration of Human Rights and its covenants. Basically, however, human rights are those rights human beings have simply because they are human beings and not because they are members of a particular nation or state. The Universal Declaration of Human Rights has become a standard against which we can measure the treatment of citizens by a government, and most authors use this standard in their writings on human rights. Some of the literature, particularly the more philosophical writings, reflects differences in interpretation, mainly between East and West, but also differences in how human rights should be implemented.

These differences occur not only among nations but within the same country, as could be seen quite clearly in the United States by contrasting the approaches taken by the Carter and Reagan administrations to the role of human rights in foreign policy. Carter stated he would make human rights the "soul" of his foreign policy and attempted to do so by withholding economic and other aid from those countries involved in gross human rights violations. The Reagan administration, on the other hand, pursued a policy of "quiet diplomacy"—censuring or encouraging governments through private communication. Most human rights groups criticized this approach as a ploy to emphasize Soviet bloc violations while ignoring abuses by U.S. allies. They also pointed out that the Reagan policy chose to exclude economic and social rights from its consideration of basic human rights.

While the differences in perception and interpretation between East and West and among and within nations are reflected in the literature and other materials on human rights, the particular opinions of authors, editors, and others were not a factor in selecting works for this handbook. The primary purpose of this volume is to bring together those materials on human rights that would be useful to researchers, teachers, students, activists, and others interested in the subject, without regard for political or any other perspective.

Organizations committed to human rights advocacy are listed and described in Chapter 4. They include international, national, and regional groups, most of which have publications available in the United States. An attempt was made to include all such groups, but it is acknowledged that some may have been omitted, either because up-to-date information could not be found or because they did not respond to an inquiry that requested information.

Since there is a considerable amount of print and nonprint material on human rights, this handbook is necessarily limited in its scope. Except for some basic reference tools, most works cover the period of 1983–1988. Useful earlier works can be found in the bibliographies listed. The focus is on human rights in general; no attempt was made to cover works on specific rights, e.g., women's rights, minority rights, or children's rights, unless they are from a human rights perspective. Works considered to be primarily on civil rights were also excluded, as were technical works on international law.

Since the book is intended for researchers, students, and activists, an important consideration was whether the material is likely to be available in academic or public libraries or directly from a publisher or producer. The books and periodicals selected include a range from the popular to the scholarly, but much information will be found only in journal articles, which can be accessed through indexes or online systems, both of which are listed. Prices for both print and nonprint resources are included when available, but readers should be aware that these are subject to change.

Chapter 5, "Books and Periodicals," is arranged with reference tools, most of which are specific to human rights, first, followed by monographs and periodicals. Chapter 6 covers nonprint media, computer networks, and databases. Nonprint materials can be invaluable for teachers and those who plan programs or small group discussions on human rights. Those listed are meant to be samples of the types of materials available. Little is found on human rights in general; most audiovisual materials focus on one or another right, or more frequently, on the deprivation of specific rights. Included is a list of producers and distributors that should facilitate locating needed material of this type. Databases and computer networks, though few exist in this field at the present time, can be very valuable and should become more readily accessible in the future.

Two other chapters, 2 and 3, are the chronology and a selection of biographical sketches. The chronology lists some of the key dates and events in the development of human rights in our time. The biographical material is included primarily for students and those who might be unfamiliar with names in human rights literature. This section attempts to provide examples of those who have been active in promoting human rights or have been victims of human rights abuse. People included have appeared in news articles or were suggested by those active in human rights work, though it should be noted that those who do the real work of preserving human rights are most often unknown—peasants in countries where speaking out for labor rights is likely to bring torture or death, doctors and lawyers who jeopardize their careers and sometimes their lives by refusing to cooperate with illegal and inhumane treatment of ordinary citizens, and the men and women representing various religious groups who have spent years of their lives working to maintain basic human rights for the poor and neglected in society. For this reason it is never possible to have an adequate list of those prominent in the field.

The final chapter contains copies of the International Bill of Human Rights and some of the other documents important to the study of human rights. As with selection for other chapters, it was difficult to make choices. What is important for one is less important for another. Since human rights is not an academic field in the same way political science or nuclear physics is, there will always be questions about why some materials are selected and others are not. This work is meant to be an introduction; it is hoped that users will make suggestions for additions, deletions, and changes.

I am particularly grateful to David Hinkley, Western Regional Director of Amnesty International, for his willingness to do the Introduction during a very busy time. He has given an excellent overview of the importance of human rights in our time. My thanks go also to the many librarians, particularly at the University of California at Los Angeles, the University of Southern California, and the California State University at Los Angeles—Suzanne Sullivan, especially—who were so helpful; to the many individuals who responded so courteously to my letters and phone calls; and finally to my family and to my colleagues at Immaculate Heart College Center, particularly Teresa Hudock for her assistance with computer problems and Mary Nakagawa, our library assistant, for much support and encouragement.

The shortcomings of the work are entirely mine, but I hope that in spite of them, it will be useful to those who in whatever way dedicate themselves to the promotion of human rights throughout the world.

Lucille Whalen
Immaculate Heart College Center
Los Angeles

1

Introduction

David Hinkley
Western Regional Director, Amnesty International

WHEN THE MEMBER STATES of the fledgling United Nations proclaimed, on December 10, 1948, the Universal Declaration of Human Rights, only the visionaries among them could have foreseen the profound developments and remarkable achievements that would result from their historic action. For in a mere 40 years, the concept of international responsibility and accountability for protection of fundamental human rights has taken root in an astonishing array of laws, covenants, institutions, popular movements, and countless intercessions on behalf of victims of injustice the world over.

During the same 40-year period, however, the very rights proclaimed in the Universal Declaration have suffered unspeakable abuses on a scale rivaling history's worst atrocities. And though ideology has often been the foundation, or at least the rationale, for such depredations, no system of government has proven to be immune to the abuses of power that result in torture, unjust imprisonment, and political killings on every continent.

The simultaneous flowering of the modern human rights movement and the global epidemic of systematic abuse is more than a historical irony. It is instead an intensifying moral conflict of two tendencies that cannot permanently coexist.

The roots of the conflict are as ancient as human social organization and as basic as the clash between unbridled lust for power and instinctive longing for justice and fair play. But a century of global wars and conflicts—military and economic, "hot" and "cold," East vs. West, and North vs. South—together with the accelerating impact of revolutionary communications, travel, and technological advancements, has begun to crystallize an awareness of global interdependency whose progress is irreversible.

The postwar human rights movement springs directly from such an awareness. Pogroms, genocides, and the rising tide of torture—now systematic in a third of the world's nations—defy its meaning. Such abuses by armies, police forces, and security agencies and the proliferation of "death squads," vigilante and clandestine forces that work the will of despotic governments stand increasingly naked in the light of determined investigation by human rights monitors. As laws, institutions, and human rights constituencies spread, the consequences for human rights violators grow more serious and their efforts to evade accountability, including increasing attacks on those who expose them, grow more devious, determined, and savage.

Emerging from the ashes of World War II, writer Albert Camus said, "A great unequal battle has begun, between the forces of dialogue and the forces of terror." That is perhaps as good a definition as any for the modern human rights struggle.

The Universal Declaration of Human Rights has 30 articles that together define a global consensus, in principle though not in practice, concerning the fundamental rights every human being is endowed with and which every government must respect, preserve, and promote. Examples are the right to life and security of the person; the right to be free from torture and cruel, inhuman, and degrading treatment or punishment; and the rights to free speech, association, religious belief, equal protection before the law, freedom of movement, privacy, free choice of employment, education, and social security.

Some of the articles are aimed at restricting the authority and uses of power available to governments. Others prescribe the obligations of governments toward their citizens. No rank or priority is assigned to the articles within the declaration or to the covenants, conventions, and protocols that have been promulgated in order to give its principles the force of international law. All the articles were conceived as essential and universal by the drafters, led by Eleanor Roosevelt, who was then the U.S. delegate to the United Nations Human Rights Commission and its chairperson.

Before 1948, traditional diplomacy had never included discussions between governments about the domestic policies affecting human rights observance of either party, particularly between friendly governments. Such matters were regarded as the internal concerns of the countries involved. For allies to criticize the human rights record of their diplomatic and economic partners was nearly unthinkable, a breach that could only be expected to damage friendly relations. Indeed, no single standard for what represents the rights of citizens everywhere could have been cited. The Universal Declaration of Human Rights not only established that single, global standard, its very existence was predicated on the concept that fundamental rights are the proper concern of all people regardless of boundaries. No less important than their endorsement of the articles themselves was their embracing the concept of international accountability by the Declaration's signatories, which includes every member state in the United Nations.

Another early human rights visionary, René Cassin, told activists in Paris at the time the Declaration was signed that, significant as it was as a foundation for future efforts to protect human rights, it would prove futile unless its principles were actively fostered by an informed constituency committed to investigating abuses and demanding redress and prevention the world over.

Cassin's observation has been borne out in the ensuing four decades. Old habits of strident ideological posturing between adversarial governments and diffidence among allies remained the rule. Vested interests and political trade-offs within intergovernmental bodies inhibited effective action even in the most extreme human rights emergencies.

No example is more illustrative of this failure than the lack of response by the United Nations to the wave of genocidal killings that swept Cambodia between 1975 and 1979. Reliable estimates of the toll in human life of the policies of the Khmer Rouge government of Pol Pot have reached into the millions. Yet nearly a decade later, there has not been a single vote of censure, not even an acknowledgment of the fact that an atrocity of historic magnitude was carried out in Cambodia, in any intergovernmental body.

By contrast, when thousands of Argentinian citizens were abducted and caused to "disappear" during the so-called dirty war in the late 1970s, the force of world opinion was galvanized by the heroic witness of a group of relatives of the missing. The "Madres de Plaza de Mayo" demonstrated weekly in Buenos Aires in defiance of threats, harassment, arrests, and intimidatory acts by Argentine officials. Other domestic groups, including the Permanent Assembly on Human Rights, courageously published well-documented accounts and figures on "disappearances." International organizations like Amnesty International campaigned vigorously for an end to the terror against presumed opponents of the military government.

These activities led in turn to intergovernmental action. The Inter-American Commission of the Organization of American States sent a fact-finding team to Argentina in 1979 and filed a devastating report the following year. Argentina was the focus of the first report of the United Nations Working Group on Enforced and Involuntary "Disappearances," one of the many vitally important agencies created to implement the U.N.'s growing human rights agenda. Though it was a change of government that brought an end to systematic human rights abuses in Argentina, worldwide attention to the problem of "disappearances" had an inhibiting effect on these abuses, and this was demonstrable even before the return to democracy.

In the absence of global outcry, massive human rights violations in Pol Pot's Cambodia remain unredressed. Many other crises have suffered from neglect, sparse or fickle attention from international news media, and insufficient or ineffective response from governments and world opinion. Thousands have been executed after summary trials in Iran since Ayatollah Khomeini came to power in 1979. Despite countless humanitarian appeals, there is little evidence of sensitivity to outside pressure, and in late 1988 increased opposition activity was met with yet another wave of executions and torture.

Such intransigence poses special challenges to the concept of international responsibility for human rights protection, as it demonstrates the urgent need for growth in the size and clout of the human rights movement and for more effective enforcement machinery within intergovernmental bodies.

Even so, the early growth of the young movement has been explosive. In the 1980s, over a thousand human rights monitoring groups have sprung up throughout the world. From the Philippines to South Africa, from El Salvador to Czechoslovakia, their accomplishments have been historic, the more remarkable because of persistent, often brutal interference with their activities from the governments whose policies they have exposed and denounced.

Sudden, dramatic results are rare. But the cumulative effect of years of persistent and escalating activity can be and has been profound. Perhaps no example is more widely publicized than the changes that have begun in the Soviet Union. An untold number of political prisoners were held in deplorable conditions in what writer Aleksandr Solzhenitsyn called "the Gulag Archipelago," a vast network of labor camps, prisons, and penal colonies from the Ukraine to Siberia. Torture was systematic, and Soviet officials locked political suspects in special psychiatric units where use of psychotropic drugs and close confinement with the criminally insane were commonplace.

Courageous activists like Andrei Sakharov and publishers of the underground *samizdat* accounts of human rights abuses drew global attention. The World Psychiatric Association's searching criticism of Soviet abuse of psychiatry led to a walkout of the WPA by the Soviets, reflecting a level of sensitivity which has increased still more in the age of *glasnost*. In 1988, administration of psychiatric procedures was shifted from the Justice to the Health Ministry in what may prove a crucial structural reform. In the same period, hundreds of prisoners of conscience have been released, including a growing number held in psychiatric detention. A public discussion of reforming the most sweeping provisions of the criminal code, those which have been most often used to justify the detention of political prisoners, is underway; public debate and writing calling for restriction or abolition of the death penalty is being tolerated for the first time in decades.

It seems unlikely that even a reform-minded leader could have achieved such results without the history of domestic and international activism contributing to the impetus for change. It remains an open question whether the hundreds of remaining prisoners of conscience will benefit and whether the administrative reforms will be institutionalized in law and practice. But the recognition that even a superpower is susceptive to the determined outcry of an informed world public offers tremendous promise for the future.

In the United States, public awareness and governmental policy in the human rights arena evolved dramatically in the 1970s. Though the most visible benchmark was the presidential leadership of Jimmy Carter, who declared human rights the "soul of U.S.

foreign policy" and placed the issue squarely onto the mainstream media and public agenda, the modern human rights movement in the United States has many antecedents and benefactors.

Rooted in the philosophy of the Enlightenment, the Founding Fathers produced some of the most important human rights documents in history, building the concept of inalienable rights into the Declaration of Independence and the Constitution. In the nineteenth century, abolitionists mounted a movement to eradicate slavery that, though scoffed at by "realists" who believed slavery and the slave trade ineradicable, made an enormous contribution to the process that deposited the slave block on the same historical waste heap on which activists today aspire to dump the torture rack and the electric chair.

The Depression of the 1930s led to government programs designed to deliver the social and economic obligations of government to the poor and disenfranchised that are now reflected in such articles of the Universal Declaration of Human Rights as those requiring free choice of employment, social security, access to trade unionism, and assistance in the event of unemployment or disability.

The civil rights, civil liberties, and rights of women movements of the 1950s, 1960s, and 1970s created a consciousness of a body of rights that had long been denied to many Americans, demonstrating forcefully that laws and institutions alone, without vigilance and when necessary militant agitation by a concerned constituency, cannot guarantee observance of fundamental rights, even in a democracy.

Even before President Carter's pronouncements on human rights, the U.S. Congress had taken important steps in the 1970s to make international human rights a regular feature of foreign policy. Congressman Donald Fraser of Minnesota, for example, spearheaded a drive to require the U.S. State Department to report annually to Congress on human rights conditions in every country in the world. Additional legislation linked such policies as Most Favored Nation status (governing tariff limitations), military aid, loans through international financial institutions, and supply of police and security equipment, to the human rights performance of recipient nations. President Carter instituted a Department of Human Rights and Humanitarian Affairs in the State Department to foster compliance with the new legislation and further institutionalize the place of human rights concerns in overall U.S. policy.

Meanwhile, human rights organizations such as Amnesty International, Human Rights Watch, the Lawyers Committee for Human Rights, and numerous others have proliferated and flourished through the generosity and growing activism of a burgeoning constituency of concerned Americans.

Looking forward to the 40 years to come can be, by turns, daunting and exhilarating. The failures, shortcomings, and immense obstacles experienced in the generation since the signing of the Universal Declaration of Human Rights should never be underestimated. Censorship, illiteracy, government attacks on human rights monitors, cynicism, and deal-making in the councils of power will not be surmounted by the committed few. The movement for human rights must become truly global, carried forward by the millions rather than by the thousands of people, if such barriers are to be surmounted.

But the experience of achievement in adversity and astonishing growth since 1948 provides legitimate reason for hope that the aspirations of the human rights constituency—such goals as making torture "as unthinkable as slavery"—may be within reach.

2

Chronology

THE IDEA OF FUNDAMENTAL RIGHTS and freedoms has existed since at least Old Testament times. Magna Carta, the English Bill of Rights, the Declaration of Independence, the French Declaration of the Rights of Man and Citizen, and the League of Nations Covenant all expressed ideas of inalienable, universal rights. It was not until the 1940s, however—particularly at the time of the founding of the United Nations—that the modern concept of human rights came into existence. The idea of international law protecting the rights of individuals and not only states was a new one, brought about by the horrors of World War II. Thus the highlights in the development of human rights for the most part have been the various declarations and covenants to which nations of the world subscribe. It should be pointed out that the declarations and resolutions are generally statements on which nations agree, but they do not have the force of law, while covenants, conventions, and treaties, used somewhat interchangeably, become international law when ratified by a specific number of nations. The following chronology shows the dates of the major human rights documents and events.

1941   President Franklin Roosevelt's State of the Union message includes one of the first references to the "Four Freedoms"—freedom of speech, freedom of religion, freedom from want and freedom from fear—freedoms which, he states, should prevail everywhere in the world.

1944   Declaration of Philadelphia. Two famous passages incorporated into the Constitution of the International Labour Organisation (ILO), a specialized agency of the U.N.: "All human beings, irrespective of race, creed, or sex, have the right to pursue both their material well-being and their spiritual development in conditions of freedom and dignity, of economic security, and equal opportunity"; and "Freedom of expression and association are essential to sustained progress."

1945   Preamble to the U.N. Charter. Includes the phrase "to reaffirm faith in fundamental human rights, in the dignity and worth of the human person, in the equal rights of men and women, and of nations large and small"—one of the first times human rights is mentioned in an international treaty.

1946   U.N. General Assembly approves and ratifies Nuremberg Principles, which establish the right and authority of nations to punish violators of human rights and specify that soldiers may not be acquitted on the grounds of following orders of superiors when they violate the rules of war.

1948   U.N. General Assembly adopts Universal Declaration of Human Rights, which prescribes that all human beings are entitled to all human rights and fundamental freedoms set forth in the declaration. This is the most fundamental of all U.N. instruments; most subsequent human rights statements are based on its tenets.

Convention on the Prevention and Punishment of the Crime of Genocide. Recognizes genocide as a crime under international law and states that those accused of it, in wartime or peace, can be tried by the country where the crime was committed or by such international tribunals as have jurisdiction.

1949   American Declaration of the Rights and Duties of Man, based on the Universal Declaration of Human Rights, brought into existence by the Organization of American States (OAS) in Bogotá and adopted for Latin America.

Council of Europe established. Its statutes include the statement, "Every member of the Council of Europe must accept the principles of the rule of law and of the enjoyment by all persons within its jurisdiction of human rights and fundamental freedoms." It also proposes establishment of an internal organization to ensure the collective guarantee of human rights.

1949   The Geneva Conventions. The four conventions represent a
cont.   significant attempt to protect war victims. They expressly
prohibit violence to life and person, in particular, torture,
mutilation, or cruel treatment, the taking of hostages, or any
degrading treatment. They also oblige each party to search for
those who have committed these abuses.

International Labour Organization (ILO) adopts the Right to
Organise and Collective Bargaining Convention, prescribing
for workers adequate protection against antiunion discrimination in respect of their employment.

1950   Convention for the Suppression of the Traffic in Persons and
of the Exploitation of the Prostitution of Others. Convention
parties agree to punish any person who, to gratify another,
procures, entices, or leads away, for the purpose of prostitution, another person, even with that person's consent, or
exploits the prostitution of another person, even with the
person's consent.

1951   Convention relating to the Status of Refugees. Parties agree to
give refugees "national treatment"—that is, treatment at least as
favorable as that accorded their own nationals with regard to
such rights as freedom of religion, access to courts, elementary
education, and public relief. (Convention covers only persons
who became refugees as a result of events occurring before
January 1, 1951.)

1952   Convention on the International Right of Correction. Provides
that when a signatory state finds a news report filed between
countries or disseminated abroad capable of damaging its
foreign relations or national prestige, that state may submit its
version of the facts to any other states where the report became
publicized, and that these other states are obliged to release
such a communiqué to news media within their territories.

1953   European Convention for the Protection of Human Rights and
Fundamental Freedoms. Requires contracting states to make
their laws conform to the provisions of the convention and
creates the European Court of Human Rights.

1955   Standard Minimum Rules for the Treatment of Prisoners.
These seek to set standards for acceptable treatment of prisoners and management of penal institutions.

1956   Supplementary Convention on the Abolition of Slavery, the Slave Trade, and Institutions and Practices Similar to Slavery. Requires parties to expedite, through legislative and other measures, the complete abolition of such practices as debt bondage, serfdom, and the use of a woman, without the right to refuse, as an object of barter in marriage.

1957   Convention on the Nationality of Married Women. Contracting states agree that neither celebration nor dissolution of marriage between a national and an alien can automatically affect the nationality of the wife.

Convention concerning the Abolition of Forced Labour (ILO). Members agree not to use any form of forced or compulsory labor as a means of political coercion or education or as punishment for holding political views ideologically opposed to the established system.

1958   Discrimination (Employment and Occupation) Convention (ILO). Each ratifying member agrees to declare and pursue a national policy promoting equal opportunity and treatment in employment and occupation, with a view to eliminating any discrimination in respect thereof.

1959   The Organization of American States (OAS) creates the Inter-American Commission on Human Rights to promote respect for human rights. The commission asserts its authority to study the human rights situations of member states.

Declaration of the Rights of the Child. Maintains that children shall enjoy special protection and be given opportunities and facilities, by law and other means, to enable them to develop physically, mentally, morally, spiritually, and socially in a healthy and normal manner in conditions of freedom and dignity.

1960   Convention against Discrimination in Education (UNESCO). Parties agree to ensure, by legislation where necessary, that there is no discrimination in the admission of pupils to educational institutions; to make primary education free and compulsory; to make secondary education generally available and accessible to all, and higher education equally accessible to all on the basis of individual capacity; and to make certain that the factors relating to the quality of education provided are equivalent in all public education.

1961 Convention on the Reduction of Statelessness. Specifies grounds on which a state may not deprive a person of nationality; these include racial, ethnic, religious, or political reasons.

1962 Convention on Consent to Marriage, Minimum Age for Marriage and Registration of Marriages. States must take legislative action to specify a minimum age for marriage and to provide for the registration of marriages by an appropriate official. Marriages may not be legally entered into without the full and free consent of both parties.

1963 Declaration on the Elimination of All Forms of Racial Discrimination. Discrimination against human beings on the grounds of race, color, or ethnic origin is an offense to human dignity and shall be condemned as a denial of the principles of the Charter of the U.N., as a violation of the fundamental freedoms proclaimed in the Universal Declaration of Human Rights, and as an obstacle to friendly and peaceful relations among nations. Special measures shall be taken in appropriate circumstances to secure adequate protection of individuals belonging to certain racial groups, but these measures may not include the maintenance of unequal or separate rights for different racial groups.

1964 Employment Policy Convention (ILO). States that parties must declare and pursue, as a major goal, an active policy designed to promote full, productive, and freely chosen employment.

Civil Rights Act of 1964. Signed by President Lyndon B. Johnson, the act is a landmark in the development of full human rights for all citizens in the United States.

1965 International Convention on the Elimination of All Forms of Racial Discrimination. States condemn racial discrimination and undertake to pursue by all appropriate means and without delay a policy of eliminating racial discrimination in all its forms, to promote understanding among the races, and to discourage anything that tends to strengthen racial division.

1966 International Covenant on Economic, Social and Cultural Rights. States recognize rights to which all people are entitled, including the right to work, to just and favorable conditions of work, to social security, to an adequate standard of living, to the highest attainable standard of physical and mental health, to education, to take part in cultural life, and to enjoy the benefits of scientific progress.

1966 International Covenant on Civil and Political Rights. Establishes
cont. a legal obligation on states to protect the civil and political rights
of every individual, without discrimination as to race, sex,
language, or religion. It ensures the right to life, liberty, security,
individual privacy, and protection from torture and other cruel,
inhuman or degrading treatment. The covenant also guarantees
a fair trial and protection against arbitrary arrest or detention
and grants freedom of thought, conscience, and religion,
freedom of opinion and expression, and freedom of association.

Optional Protocol to the International Covenant on Civil and
Political Rights. A state party to the International Covenant that
becomes a party to the Optional Protocol recognizes the competence of the Human Rights Committee to receive and consider communications from individuals subject to its
jurisdiction who claim to be victims of a violation by the state
party of any of the rights set forth in the covenant.

1967 Declaration on the Elimination of Discrimination against
Women. All appropriate measures shall be taken to abolish
existing laws, customs, regulations, and practices that discriminate against women and to establish adequate legal protection
for equal rights of men and women.

Declaration on Territorial Asylum. Asylum granted by a state
to persons seeking asylum from political persecution shall be
respected by all other states. No such person shall be subjected
to such measures as rejection at the border, expulsion, or
compulsory return to any state where he or she may be
subjected to persecution except for overriding reasons of
national security or to safeguard the population.

Convention on the Non-Applicability of Statutory Limitations
to War Crimes and Crimes against Humanity. The convention
states principles regarding international cooperation in the
detention, arrest, extradition, and punishment of war crimes
and crimes against humanity; e.g., there is no statutory limitation on certain crimes such as genocide, eviction by armed
attack, or inhuman acts resulting from the policy of apartheid.

1969 The American Convention on Human Rights. Signed in San
José, Costa Rica, but not entered into force until 1978, this is
one of the most ambitious and far-reaching documents on
human rights issued by any international body. Among other
features, it bans the death penalty and authorizes compensation
for victims of human rights abuses in certain cases.

1969
cont.
The ILO receives the Nobel Peace Prize for its work on behalf of human rights. The ILO was the first international governmental agency, under the League of Nations, to define and vindicate human rights. It has sought tirelessly to improve the conditions of working men and women around the world.

1971
Declaration of the Rights of Mentally Retarded Persons. The mentally retarded person has, to the maximum degree of feasibility, the same rights as other human beings, including the right to proper medical care, to educational training, to economic security, and to a decent standard of living.

Workers' Representatives Convention (ILO). Workers' representatives shall enjoy effective protection against any act prejudicial to them, including dismissal, based on their participation in union activities, insofar as they act in conformity with existing laws or other jointly agreed-upon arrangements.

1973
International Convention on the Suppression and Punishment of the Crime of Apartheid. Inhuman acts resulting from the policies and practices of apartheid and similar policies of racial segregation and discrimination are crimes that violate the principles of international law and constitute a serious threat to international peace and security.

1974
Universal Declaration on the Eradication of Hunger and Malnutrition (World Health Conference). All men, women, and children have the inalienable right to be free from hunger and malnutrition in order to develop fully and maintain their physical and mental faculties. The eradication of hunger is a common objective of all countries, especially of those in a position to help in its eradication.

Declaration on the Protection of Women and Children in Emergency and Armed Conflict. All states involved in armed conflict or in military operations either in a foreign country or in territories still under colonial domination must make special efforts to spare women and children from the ravages of war.

1975
The Helsinki Agreement or the Final Act of the Conference on Security and Co-operation in Europe. Signed in Helsinki by 33 nations and the 2 superpowers—the United States and the Soviet Union—the Helsinki accords, as they came to be called, pledged respect for human rights and fundamental freedoms, including the freedom of thought, conscience, religion or

1975
cont.
belief, for all people without distinctions as to race, sex, language, or religion. The signatories agreed to promote universal and effective respect for human rights, jointly and separately, including cooperation with the U.N.

Declaration on the Use of Scientific and Technological Progress in the Interests of Peace and for the Benefit of Mankind. States that the results of scientific and technological developments are to be used in the interests of strengthening international peace and security and for the economic and social development of peoples in accordance with the Charter of the U.N.

Declaration on the Rights of Disabled Persons. States shall protect disabled persons against all exploitation, all regulations, and all treatment of a discriminatory, abusive, or degrading nature.

Declaration on the Protection of All Persons from Being Subjected to Torture and Other Cruel, Inhuman or Degrading Treatment or Punishment. No state may permit or tolerate torture or other cruel, inhuman, or degrading treatment or punishment. Exceptional circumstances such as a state of war, internal political instability, or other public emergency may not be used as a justification for such treatment.

International Women's Year and the First World Conference for the Decade for Women in Mexico City. Marks the beginning of the most profound consideration of women's rights on a worldwide basis that has ever taken place.

1977
Carter Administration emphasizes human rights. In his inaugural address, President Jimmy Carter makes it clear that human rights will be an important factor in U.S. foreign policy. In a speech to the U.N. two months later, he states that he will recommend the ratification of the major human rights treaties. Although he keeps his promise, the human rights treaties are not ratified by the United States. He does, however, create the Bureau of Human Rights and Humanitarian Affairs and appoints Patricia Derian to head the bureau.

1978
Declaration on Race and Racial Prejudice (UNESCO). All individuals and groups have the right to be different, but this right and the diversity in life-styles may not, in any circumstances, be used as a pretext for racial prejudice and may not either in law or in fact justify discriminatory practices.

1978
cont. Declaration on Fundamental Principles concerning the Contribution of the Mass Media to Strengthening Peace and International Understanding, to the Promotion of Human Rights and to Countering Racialism, Apartheid and Incitement to War (UNESCO). Journalists must have access to public information for reporting so that individuals may have a diversity of sources from which to check the accuracy of facts and appraise events objectively.

1979 Code of Conduct for Law Enforcement Officials. In the performance of their duties, law enforcement officials shall respect and protect human dignity and maintain and uphold the human rights of all persons. They may use force only when strictly necessary and to the extent required for the performance of their duty. They may never inflict, instigate, or tolerate any act of torture or other cruel, inhuman, or degrading treatment, nor invoke superior orders or exceptional circumstances as a justification for such treatment.

Convention on the Elimination of All Forms of Discrimination against Women. Parties shall take all appropriate measures, including legislation, to ensure the full development and advancement of women, for the purpose of guaranteeing them the exercise of human rights on a basis of equality with men.

1980 Second World Conference for the Decade for Women. Conference held in Copenhagen to assess the progress made in implementing the 1975 Mexico City conference's plan of action and to adopt guidelines for international, regional, and national efforts to assist women in attaining equality in all spheres of life as part of a plan of action for the second half of the decade.

1981 UNESCO Meeting in Freetown, Sierra Leone. A meeting of experts to analyze the forms of individual and collective action by which human rights violations can be combatted.

African Charter on Human and People's Rights. At a meeting of the Organization of African Unity (OAU), the leaders of 51 member states adopted the African Charter on Human and People's Rights. The charter reiterates the basic principles of human rights and stresses decolonization and the elimination of apartheid as top priorities. It seeks to preserve the traditional African social concept that the individual is not considered independent from society but is subordinate to the group.

1981   Declaration on the Elimination of All Forms of Intolerance and
cont.   of Discrimination Based on Religion or Belief. All persons shall
have the right to have a religion or belief of their choice, and
shall have the freedom, either individually or in community
with others and in public or private, to manifest their religion
or belief in worship, observance, practice, and teaching.

The Universal Islamic Declaration of Human Rights. Many of
the provisions of this declaration are similar to those in other
major human rights instruments; the declaration contains
references to the right to life, to freedom under the law, to
equality before the law, to fair trial, and to freedom from
torture. Its basis is religious rather than regional and draws
justification from reference to the Koran and the *sunna*.

1982   Principles of Medical Ethics. Health personnel, particularly
physicians, charged with the medical care of prisoners and
detainees have a duty to provide for them the same standard
and quality of physical and mental health care afforded others.
It is a gross violation of medical ethics to engage actively or
passively in acts that constitute participation in or complicity
with torture or other cruel, inhuman, or degrading treatment
or punishment.

1984   Convention against Torture and Other Cruel, Inhuman or
Degrading Treatment or Punishment. Defines torture as any
act by which severe physical or mental pain or suffering is
intentionally inflicted by, at the instigation of, or with the
acquiescence of someone acting in an official capacity, whether
to obtain information or confession; to punish, intimidate, or
coerce; or for reasons based on discrimination. States parties
must prevent torture in their jurisdictions and ensure that it is
legally punishable.

1985   Third World Conference for the Decade for Women. Held in
Nairobi in July 1985 to assess the progress achieved and
obstacles encountered during the past decade and to formulate
strategies for the advancement of women to implement
through the year 2000 and beyond.

1988   Almost 40 years after the U.N. approves the Genocide Convention, President Reagan signs legislation enabling the United
States to become the 98th nation to ratify the agreement. The
legislation amends the Criminal Code of the United States to
make genocide a federal offense.

3

Biographical Sketches

IT WOULD BE FOOLHARDY for anyone to presume to select individuals prominent in the human rights arena in the same way one might select those prominent in a well-defined academic area. Indeed, it is impossible to select them at all, as many of those who are doing the most to further the cause of human rights are ordinary citizens of countries where abuses abound and do so with considerable risk to themselves and their families. They are largely unknown, as are many in the United States who quietly and conscientiously work for the release of prisoners of conscience or work to change repressive laws. Nevertheless, there are individuals, known nationally or internationally, who have achieved some success in the promotion of human rights and who serve as role models for others. The following are biographical sketches of a few of these persons.

Jimmy Carter

Jimmy Carter, the 39th president of the United States, serving from 1977 to 1981, will be remembered in history as a president who made human rights an integral part of his administration's foreign policy. The facts of Carter's life are well known—he was a Baptist fundamentalist, a peanut farmer, and one-term governor of Georgia before becoming president. Born in Plains, Georgia, on October 1, 1924, he grew up in that area, attended Georgia Tech and the U.S. Naval Academy, from which he graduated in 1946. He spent some time on battleships and in the submarine service before being accepted into the nuclear submarine program.

When his father died in 1953, Carter returned to take over the family business in Plains and became active in church and community affairs. It was during this time that he began his human rights advocacy. At one time, having refused to join the local White Citizens Council, he found his businesses were boycotted. On another occasion he and his family and one other person were the only ones in his church to vote against a resolution refusing blacks and civil rights "agitators" the right to worship in the church.

During his political career Carter served as a senator and later as governor of Georgia, which gave him an opportunity to open up government positions for women and blacks and set in motion several humanitarian programs. During his primary campaign for the presidency, Carter focused on human rights in many of his foreign policy statements and made it an issue in the debates during the general election campaign. It was one of the factors that stirred enthusiasm for his campaign among young people, church-affiliated groups, broad-based citizen groups, and even some labor groups.

It was not surprising that Carter, on taking the oath of office, pledged, "Because we are free, we can never be indifferent to the facts of freedom elsewhere. Our moral sense dictates a clear-cut preference for those societies which share with us an abiding respect for individual human rights." Nor was it surprising that one of the first steps taken by the new administration was the appointment of Patricia Derian, a long-time civil rights activist from the South, as head of the newly established Bureau of Human Rights and Humanitarian Affairs.

As a result of this human rights policy, the United States opposed many loans to foreign countries on human rights grounds, arms transfer proposals to a dozen countries were altered, and diplomatic dialogue on human rights occurred on many levels. Some of the other stands Carter took on human and civil rights issues were his support for the Equal Rights Amendment, universal voter registration, granting pardons to the Vietnam War draft resisters, and ending a practice of denying visitors' visas to foreign Communists wishing to visit the United States. These and other factors were the reasons the International League for Human Rights in its report cited President

Carter's policies as being responsible for significant improvement in human rights around the world.

Patricia M. Derian

Patricia Murphy Derian, a Washington, D.C., writer, was born in New York in 1929. After attending Palos Verdes College, Millsaps College, and the University of Virginia School of Nursing, she became involved in politics and held many government and political positions, including that of consultant for the Office of Economic Opportunity and the Head Start Program, Democratic National committeewoman, and vice-chairperson of the Mississippi State Democratic Party. Very active in women's affairs, she was a member of the steering committee of the Democratic National Committee Women's Caucus and a member of Democratic Women for Affirmative Action. Her work as deputy director of the Carter-Mondale National Campaign and on the Carter-Mondale Transition Team in 1976 was perhaps instrumental in President Jimmy Carter's appointing her the first head of the newly created Bureau of Human Rights and Humanitarian Affairs. While she held this position, Derian worked long and hard to make human rights considerations an integral part of U.S. foreign policy—a goal Carter had stated would be an essential part of his administration. Since completing her term of office, she has remained involved in human rights issues, as evidenced by her work on the boards of the Fund for Free Expression, Human Rights Internet, and Americas Watch. Derian continues to speak out on human rights issues whenever possible.

Vaclav Havel

Born in Prague on October 5, 1936, Vaclav Havel is a Czech playwright who has used his dramatic skills to further the cause of human rights. When the Communist government nationalized industry in Czechoslovakia in 1948, Havel's parents were forced to give up their property and business and take low-paying jobs. This turn of events also denied easy access to an education for their son, but he managed by working days and continuing his schooling nights to receive his education at a technical college and then the Prague Academy of the Arts. After doing his compulsory military service in the late 1950s, Havel worked as a stagehand, electrician, secretary, and manuscript reader before becoming a playwright in the early 1960s. In his many plays, he frequently tried to show the dehumanizing effects of mechanization on society and the individual spirit.

When the Soviet Union, along with other Warsaw Pact armies, invaded Czechoslovakia in 1968, Havel addressed groups of Czech artists and writers from an underground radio station, urging them to unite in the cause of human rights. He was able to convince a small group to commit themselves to use whatever means they could to protest repression by the government. Havel's plays and writings were subsequently banned and he was twice imprisoned for his human rights advocacy. In 1977 Havel signed Charter 77, a document protesting the failure of the Czechoslovakian Socialist Republic to abide by the Helsinki Covenant on Civil and Political Rights, which it had signed. The government's response was to arrest large numbers of those who had signed the document, among them Havel, who had been one of the three elected spokesmen for the protest. He was jailed for four months and later brought to trial for sending copies of his banned writings out of the country for publication. Though given a suspended sentence, he later founded a movement known as the Committee for the Defense of the Unjustly Persecuted, and along with six others was sentenced to four and one-half years at hard labor.

Though known principally for his plays—*The Memorandum*, a full-length play satirizing official gibberish, and three one-act plays about conformists trying to rationalize their collusion with a corrupt system (*Interview, A Private View,* and *Protest*) are regarded as his best—Havel has had a profound influence on human rights, particularly the right of artists and intellectuals to criticize the government in their works.

John G. Healey

Born in Pittsburgh in 1938 of a schoolteacher mother and metallurgist father, John Healey grew up with a keen sense of justice. After receiving his B.A. degree from St. Fidelis College in Pennsylvania and his M.A. degree from the Capuchin College in Washington, D.C., Healey was ordained a priest in 1966. Following his ordination, he taught at the Catholic University in Washington, D.C., and served for a time in a Maryland parish. During this time he became active in civil rights and antiwar demonstrations. In 1969 he left the priesthood and became director of the American Freedom From Hunger Foundation, where he was successful not only in raising funds for the foundation but in raising awareness of the hunger problem.

From 1974 to 1977, he was program officer for the Center for Community Change. In 1977 President Jimmy Carter appointed him director of the Peace Corps in Lesotho. While he held this post, he saw firsthand the important work of Amnesty International, and in 1981 he left the Peace Corps to become executive director of Amnesty International U.S.A. in New York.

With Healey's intense concern for human rights and the administrative skills he brought to the office, Amnesty in the United States became the largest branch of the worldwide organization. Its membership grew from 40,000 members when he began to over 300,000 in 1988, and the financial support grew from a $3 million annual budget to one of $15 million. More importantly, Healey has been successful in raising the awareness of thousands—especially young people—of human rights abuses throughout the world through the rock concerts he has organized. Working tirelessly for human rights, Healey has been instrumental in bringing relief to many around the world who have been victims of government human rights violations.

Juan E. Mendez

Juan Mendez, a lawyer and educator, was born and raised in Argentina, receiving his education from Stella Maris Catholic University and the Provincial University in Mar del Plata and later from the American University in Washington, D.C. He was in private law practice in Argentina from 1970 to 1975, holding the position of acting dean of the School of Economics at Provincial University for the year of 1973.

Under Argentina's state of siege, Mendez became a political prisoner without charges for 18 months. Adopted as a "Prisoner of Conscience" by Amnesty International in 1976, he was exiled in 1977. He became director of Centro Cristo Rey, a Catholic Center for Hispanics, in Aurora, Illinois, and then accepted a position with the Alien Rights Law Project under the sponsorship of the Lawyers' Committee for Civil Rights Under Law in Washington, D.C.

In 1982 Mendez became director of the Washington, D.C., office of Americas Watch, a position that has allowed him to participate in many of the Americas Watch investigations of human rights violations, particularly in Latin American countries. He has been responsible for several of the excellent Americas Watch reports and other publications on human rights in Latin American countries.

On one of his recent monitoring missions, Mendez was ordered to leave Ayacucho in Peru because he was told he did not have permission from the Politico-Military Command there to carry out such work. Since he had already received approval from the prime minister, the foreign minister, and others, he strongly protested this expulsion. It was of particular concern because during his brief stay there before the incident he received eyewitness testimony about the disappearance by the military of two men who had themselves witnessed a massacre of peasants that occurred earlier in the year. In a letter to Peruvian President Garcia Pérez, Mendez strongly protested this and other restrictions on the ability of Americas Watch to investigate allegations of human rights abuses. Mendez's activities on behalf of human rights, though less known than those of others, are nonetheless powerful in attaining human rights for many people.

Aryeh Neier

Although Aryeh Neier was born in Berlin in 1937 of parents who had come to Germany as Jewish refugees from Eastern Europe, he spent only a brief time there. Shortly before the outbreak of World War II in 1939, his parents took him and his sister to London, where they remained until they moved to New York in 1947. Several of his relatives, including three of his grandparents, died in the Holocaust.

Neier became a U.S. citizen in 1955. He obtained a degree in labor relations from Cornell University in 1958. Even as a student he was active in working for "causes"—mostly in labor union affairs. He worked for a time as a mediation and arbitration intern; with these experiences he moved easily into his first job as labor secretary with the League for Industrial Democracy. He later became executive director of the organization, and following that was an associate editor of *Current,* a public affairs journal.

Neier's work as a human rights advocate began when he took a position as a field development officer for the American Civil Liberties Union (ACLU) in 1963. He was responsible for organizing legal support for civil rights activists in the South. Much of his time in the ACLU was spent fighting for basic human rights, particularly for the poor and for minority groups. In 1965 he became the executive director of the New York ACLU, and in 1970 of the national ACLU office. During this time he championed some unpopular causes, which led to dissension both within and outside the organization, but he never veered from his positions regarding what he considered basic freedoms. One of the controversies that gained notoriety was his defense of the National Socialist Party—a neo-Nazi organization—which planned a march in Skokie, Illinois, where many of the inhabitants were Holocaust survivors. Although Neier was not without his detractors, the ACLU's membership grew and prospered under his direction. He resigned in 1978 to join the faculty of New York University as a visiting professor of law and to pursue research and writing.

Since 1978 Neier has been involved with Americas Watch and Helsinki Watch, citizens' human rights organizations. In 1981 he became the executive director of Human Rights Watch, the umbrella organization for these and Asia Watch. In this position he has extended his concern for civil rights to global human rights, being very much involved in the investigation of violations of human rights in various countries and the writing of reports on these investigations. In addition to the reports for Human Rights Watch and its constituent organizations, Neier has published many other books and articles on human rights, including *Dossier* (1975), *Crime and Punishment: A Radical Solution* (1976), *Defending My Enemy* (1979), and *Only Judgment: The Limits of Litigation in Social Change* (1982).

Adolfo Pérez Esquivel

Adolfo Pérez Esquivel, born in Argentina in 1931, became a beacon of light for the cause of human rights at a time when violence and terror were rampant in his country and rapidly spreading to other countries. After graduation from the National School of Fine Arts in Buenos Aires in 1956, he married and pursued a career as a sculptor and professor of fine arts. Although successful in his career—much of his sculpture is in the permanent collections of various museums in Argentina—he gave up this career in 1974 to devote himself to the task of coordinating various nonviolent peace and justice groups into an organization called Servicio Paz y Justicia (Service for Peace and Justice) and founding its journal, *Paz y Justicia*. Although Pérez Esquivel is a devout Roman Catholic, the organization he founded was ecumenical and not under the auspices of the Roman Catholic hierarchy, most of whom were reluctant to become involved in the political turmoil that was responsible for such grave human rights abuses.

One of the causes Pérez Esquivel took up as secretary general of the group was an international campaign to persuade the United Nations to establish a Human Rights Commission that could help bring an end to the flagrant violations of human rights not only in his country but in many others as well. He also championed the cause of the 6,000 *desaparecidos*—those who simply disappeared from their homes or off the streets of Argentine cities during the dictatorial military rule. His speaking out for such causes brought about his arrest without any legal charge and 14 months of imprisonment and torture. Even though he experienced this brutal treatment and worked to prevent it, he pointed out that peasants denied food and land also suffered grave human rights abuses. Under his leadership, Servicio Paz y Justicia sought to break the cycle of poverty that caused this type of abuse by championing the rights of workers.

In his travels throughout Latin America, he strongly supported other groups dedicated to the advancement of peace and human rights. For his efforts in this work Pérez Esquivel received the Nobel Peace Prize in 1981. In awarding the prize to a relatively unknown human rights advocate, the committee noted that Adolfo Pérez Esquivel had a message that was important and valid for the whole of Latin America.

Ginetta Sagan

One of the stories recounted often in Amnesty International literature is that of a young woman who was in a dark prison cell when a guard threw in a small round loaf of bread which she broke in two. Inside she found a matchbox that had in it a slip of paper with the word *Coraggio!* (Courage!) on it. Knowing that someone knew and cared, she nurtured the hope that was to sustain her through several more weeks of imprisonment and torture.

The woman in the story was Ginetta Sagan, a small 19-year-old at the time, who was acting as a messenger for the Italian underground during World War II. When she was caught by the police, she was subjected to all kinds of torture—rape, electric shocks, burnings, near drownings—and to the terrible realization that she was alone and no one knew she was there. Some time after the matchbox incident, when she was hardly conscious after a severe beating, she heard her captors talking about the imminent end of the war and the necessity of eliminating all witnesses. Before this could happen, however, what appeared to be two

German officers informed the Italians that she was to be taken for further questioning, but they were actually Germans in the underground who drove her to safety.

Topolina, as she was then called, spent most of the next two years in the hospital trying to recover from the physical and psychological effects of imprisonment and torture. She did recover and resolved to help others who were held prisoner for their beliefs. To this end she has worked for many years in Amnesty International U.S.A., both on the board and as an active member, and has been one of those responsible for its tremendous growth. Now living in Northern California, Sagan continues her work for human rights in the Soviet Union, Chile, Greece, Cuba, Ethiopia, Vietnam—wherever people are imprisoned for their beliefs. She insists on giving them the kind of support she received many years ago from that simple message in a matchbox—Courage!—and she spends much of her time urging others to speak out against repression in all its forms, as she is convinced that ordinary people can do much to alleviate the abuses that are still prevalent in many countries.

Andrei Sakharov

Born in Moscow in 1921, Andrei Sakharov received his B.A. degree from Moscow State University in 1942. He joined the P. N. Lebedev Physics Institute in Moscow, where he worked with Igor Tamm, who later received the Nobel Prize for Physics. Under Tamm's direction, he obtained his doctorate in physical and mathematical sciences in 1947. From then until 1956 he worked in nuclear physics as a member of a team of scientists engaged in the development of nuclear arms.

Sakharov became increasingly uneasy about "the moral problems inherent in this work" and tried unsuccessfully to bring about open discussion of these problems. In 1968 he expressed his views in an essay titled, "Progress, Peaceful Coexistence, and Intellectual Freedom," which, written from a global perspective, was an appeal to responsible citizens worldwide.

Following the publication of the essay, Sakharov was dismissed from his position at the Institute and began to have problems with the authorities. In 1970 he formed the Committee for Human Rights with friends and fellow scientists who dedicated themselves to changing the repressive measures so often taken by the government. For his work on peace and human rights issues he was awarded the Nobel Peace Prize in 1975 and took the opportunity of his Nobel lecture, which was read by his wife, Yelena Bonner, to speak about the repression in the Soviet Union and plead for restoration of human rights. In 1980 he was sent into internal exile in Gorky, where he remained until 1986, when Soviet leader Mikhail Gorbachev freed him and allowed him to return to Moscow.

Anatoly Shcharansky

A founding member of the Moscow Helsinki Watch, a group devoted to monitoring Soviet human rights violations, Anatoly Shcharansky was outspoken in his criticism of his country's repressive policies on Jewish emigration and other human rights violations. Born in Donetsk, a Ukrainian coal mining town, on January 20, 1948, Shcharansky attended school there until he left in 1966 to enroll in a special mathematics school in Moscow. He later graduated from the Moscow Physical-Technical Institute as a specialist in cybernetics and found a position as a computer specialist with the Moscow Research Institute for Oil and Gas.

Although he had a promising career, he applied for an exit visa to Israel but was refused on the grounds that his work was classified. Knowing that this was not true—the Institute was considered an "open" institution, not one involved in secret work—he began to protest the government's treatment and joined the dissident movement. With his fiancée he applied again later while imprisoned for his activities; she was granted an exit visa but he was not, though they married before she left for Israel, thinking it would be only a matter of time before he would be granted permission to emigrate.

When this permission was not forthcoming, Shcharansky became more active in the dissident movement and with a small group founded the Moscow Helsinki Watch to monitor Soviet compliance with the human rights provisions of the Helsinki Accords. He subsequently lost his job, was subject to constant threats and surveillance, and accused of being a spy for the CIA. Arrested in March of 1977 for "treasonable espionage," he was tried, found guilty, and sentenced to three years in prison to be followed by ten years in a labor camp.

Shcharansky served nine years of his thirteen-year term, suffering from long periods of isolation, hunger, and cold. His open defiance of Soviet regulations lasted until the day he left the Soviet Union as part of an exchange of prisoners. His release was due in great part to the constant support given by his wife, his family, and friends. In May of 1986 he came to America to thank the many who had supported him through his long imprisonment. He also urged the United States not only to continue "quiet diplomacy" but to put public pressure on the Soviet Union to release the thousands of Jews still awaiting exit visas.

Jacobo Timerman

Jacobo Timerman, born in the Ukraine in 1923, moved with his family to Argentina when he was five and spent most of his life there. He very early became interested in human rights issues and spent time reading socially committed writers. As a young man he was briefly arrested while attending a film sponsored by an alleged Communist group, the Argentine League for Human Rights. He became a member of the Youth League for Freedom, which supported the side of the Allies in World War II, while the government of Argentina supported the Germans. In another instance, he was briefly detained for leading an attack on the headquarters of a Nazi newspaper.

Although he attended an engineering school for a while, Timerman eventually became a journalist and also became involved at various times in radio, television, and publishing. Success in these media led to his founding his own newspaper, *La Opinión*, in 1971. Because the paper was outspoken on various issues, Timerman became a target of harassment by the government at a time when it was moving toward corruption, violence, and gross human rights violations. He was eventually imprisoned and tortured, though no charges were ever filed. Because he was well known, his case received a great deal of attention, and many human rights groups pleaded for his release. Timerman credits his release—at least partially—to the human rights policies of the United States during the Carter administration; under Carter, the United States withheld aid to Argentina because of that country's abuses.

Timerman's story is told in his book, *Prisoner without a Name, Cell without a Number*. After his release from prison, Timerman lived for a time in Israel and the United States, but he has since returned to Argentina, where he is again in the newspaper business. He, along with hundreds of others, gave testimony during the trials of the members of the military juntas responsible for so many disappearances and deaths during what has come to be called Argentina's "dirty wars," but little has been done to punish most of those responsible for the gross human rights violations of that period.

Archbishop Desmond Tutu

There has been no more forceful spokesperson against South Africa's system of apartheid than the Anglican Archbishop Desmond Mpilo Tutu. Born on October 7, 1931, in Klerksdorp, Witwatersrand, Transvaal, South Africa, Archbishop Tutu attended Bantu Normal College, from which he earned a teacher's diploma in 1953, and the University of South Africa where he received his B.A. degree the following year. After teaching for four years, he entered St. Peter's Theological College in Johannesburg, earning a Licentiate in Theology in 1960. After ordination to the priesthood in 1961 and gaining some experience as a curate, he received further degrees in theology and began a career in theological education that led eventually to his being appointed bishop of Lesotho, bishop of Johannesburg, and finally archbishop.

Although Archbishop Tutu had been keenly aware of the injustices brought about by apartheid since he was a child, it was not until he was appointed the first black to direct the South African Council of Churches that he became a leader in denouncing the government's pro-apartheid policies. He spoke out on every occasion he could about the deprivation of human rights that existed because of government policy. In 1984, when he received the Nobel Peace Prize for his heroic and fearless efforts, he used the occasion to describe the plight of black people in South Africa and did so with great eloquence. He was quick to point out, however, that in reality South Africa is a microcosm of the world and that injustice exists in many other countries. As on many occasions since then, he pleaded with the international community, and particularly the United States, to exert pressure on the South African government to end what has become a brutal system depriving thousands of their basic human rights.

Archbishop Tutu has, through the years, worked tirelessly for a nonviolent solution to the apartheid system, but he reminds the world that there are fewer and fewer who suffer under that system who believe a peaceful solution is possible. The nationwide state of emergency that exists in South Africa, imposing even further restrictions on freedoms, would seem to bear this out. Archbishop Tutu, along with representatives of other churches, was arrested in February 1988 when he participated in a peaceful demonstration against the government's banning of political activity by predominantly black organizations.

Archbishop Tutu has received many honorary degrees and awards in addition to the prestigious Nobel Peace Prize. He seizes every opportunity to describe the tragedy that exists in his country, so much of his time is spent in speaking and writing. Two of his works are *Crying in the Wilderness: The Struggle for Justice in South Africa* and *Hope and Suffering: Sermons and Speeches.*

Lech Walesa

Born in 1943, during the German occupation of Poland in World War II, Lech Walesa was educated in primary and technical schools before serving in the military for two years. Following his military service, he began work as an electrician in the Lenin shipyard in Gdansk.

In 1970 Walesa was a member of an action committee at the Lenin shipyard that encouraged rebellion against a government increase in food prices. As a result of involvement in such activities, he was dismissed in 1976 and had to rely on temporary jobs to earn a living for himself and his family. However, when increases in food prices set off further riots in 1980, Walesa joined the strikers, became head of the strike committee, and subsequently head of the Solidarity movement.

When the government was forced to negotiate with the workers, Walesa asked for certain rights—the right to form unions and the right to strike, increased wages and other benefits, and access to the broadcast media—but was careful not to go too far in demands, a decision that was not accepted by some of the more radical workers. The following year, the government outlawed Solidarity and proclaimed martial law. Walesa, along with other leaders of Solidarity, was interned for nearly a year.

In 1983 Walesa was awarded the Nobel Peace Prize in recognition of his struggle to gain basic human rights for Polish workers in spite of powerful opposition. Although he has had problems with the government in intervening years, he was allowed to leave Poland in 1988 to participate in the U.N.'s Universal Declaration of Human Rights 40th anniversary celebration held in Paris.

Elie Wiesel

Elie Wiesel, born in a small town in Romania in 1928, is well known for his indefatigable zeal in keeping before the minds of all peoples the horrors of the Holocaust. He is said to be the first to use that term in reference to the killing of some six million Jews by Nazi Germany. The only son of a shopkeeper, Wiesel was brought up with his three sisters in a deeply religious family. In spite of rumors of Nazi atrocities, the family was shocked when they, with the 15,000 other Jews in the town, were deported to the Auschwitz concentration camp in Poland. His mother and youngest sister died in the gas chambers there; he and his father were later transferred to the Buchenwald camp, from which he was liberated, but his father died there from starvation and dysentery.

Having survived the horrors of the death camps, Wiesel ended up in Paris, where he studied at the Sorbonne and eventually became a writer and journalist, a career that took him traveling to many parts of the world. He did not write about his experiences in the camps until ten years later when he published *La Nuit*, in French. It was later translated into English as *Night* but was published in the United States only after many rejections from publishers. This memoir was to be the first of many writings—novels, plays, stories, and essays—designed to raise the awareness of readers to the events of the Holocaust. After recuperating from an accident in New York, Wiesel joined the staff of a Yiddish-language newspaper there and became a U.S. citizen in 1963.

Though Wiesel's works generally focus on Jewish themes, he has at the same time shown deep concern for any violations of human rights wherever they occur. He has spoken out for the rights of black people in South Africa, of the Miskito Indians of Nicaragua, of the boat people of Indochina, of Argentine political prisoners, and of Soviet Jews. He has traveled to many of these countries to show his solidarity with oppressed peoples. For his writings and his ceaseless commitment to freedom and justice, he was awarded the Nobel Peace Prize in 1986, the most prestigious of the awards he has received through the years.

Simon Wiesenthal

Simon Wiesenthal, a prolific writer and documenter of the atrocities of the Holocaust, was born in 1908 in an Austro-Hungarian town, now part of the Ukraine. He received a degree in architectural engineering from the Technical University of Prague in 1932 and did further studies at the University of Lemberg. He was a practicing architect in Lemberg from 1939 until he was arrested in 1941. Although he escaped execution by the Nazis through the help of a former employee, he and his wife were assigned to a forced labor camp. She was later helped to escape by the underground, but Wiesenthal had to endure life in a series of concentration camps, finally being liberated by the Americans from the camp at Mauthausen.

For a time he was employed by the U.S. War Crimes Commission to help prepare evidence on Nazi atrocities, but when this position ended, he and some other volunteers established the Jewish Historical Documentation Center in Linz, Austria, to continue the gathering and preparing of evidence against Nazi war criminals. Thus began a life's work of bringing to justice those responsible for the crimes of the Holocaust. Through his efforts and that of the many volunteers who assist him, Wiesenthal has been responsible for finding and bringing to court almost 1,000 war criminals, including Adolf Eichmann, perhaps his most widely publicized case.

In addition to his work of gathering evidence that will stand up in a court of law, Wiesenthal has written many books and articles. Among his best known are *I Hunted Eichmann* (1961), *The Murderers among Us* (1967), *The Sunflower* (1969), *Sails of Hope* (1973), *The Case of Krystyna Jaworska* (1975), and *Max and Helen* (1982). His long list of honorary degrees and various awards from all over the world attests to the esteem in which Wiesenthal is held. His unflagging efforts to make the world aware of the most massive violation of human rights in modern times seem particularly important today, when there is evidence of a resurgence of Nazi terror.

4

Directory of
Organizations

THE FOLLOWING IS A SELECTED LIST of national, regional, and international organizations that have as a principal goal the preservation and promotion of human rights. Most are located in North America, and their materials are available in the United States or Canada. It should be noted that most countries and states and even some larger cities have an agency, department, or commission concerned with human rights.

African Human Rights Research Association (AHRA)
Two Assinibone Road, Suite 622
Downsview, Ontario, Canada M3J 1L1
(416) 665-8503
Munyonzwe Hamalengwa, Executive Officer

Founded in 1983 for African scholars and students and non-African specialists in African studies. The association's purpose is to promote human rights in Africa as established by the African Charter of Human and People's Rights, the Universal Declaration of Human Rights, and other international documents. Collects, publishes, and disseminates information pertaining to human rights and maintains a library on the subject.

PUBLICATIONS: *Working Papers* (a bimonthly newsletter), special bulletins, occasional monographs, and bibliographies.

Alberta Human Rights Commission
10808 99th Avenue, Room 902
Edmonton, Alberta
Canada T5K OG5
(403) 427-3116

John Lynch, Executive Director

An autonomous body established in 1973 that is responsible for the administration of the Individual's Rights Protection Act. The seven members are appointed by the Lieutenant-Governor in Council to represent the public at large. In addition to handling complaints against the act, the commission is responsible for educating the public regarding human rights issues. The commission investigates cases of discrimination relating to race, place of origin, color, religious beliefs, physical disability, age, and pregnancy, among others.

PUBLICATIONS: The commission publishes occasional educational materials and the quarterly *Alberta Human Rights Journal* (free on request).

American Civil Liberties Union (ACLU)
132 West 43rd Street
New York, NY 10036
(212) 944-9800
Ira Glasser, Executive Director

Although primarily concerned with civil rights, the ACLU works for the protection of basic human freedoms for all individuals, including children, soldiers, welfare recipients, prisoners, and mental patients. It is a network of affiliated and local chapters supported by the national office in New York, which has its own programs on litigation, legislative lobbying, and public education.

PUBLICATIONS: Maintains an extensive publication program, including newsletters, handbooks, public policy reports, and books. Some examples are *Civil Liberties*, the ACLU's quarterly newsletter (free to members); *Prison Project Journal*, a quarterly on prisoners' rights ($20); *First Principles: National Security and Civil Liberties* ($15); *Censorship News* ($25), a quarterly newsletter that reports on censorship efforts throughout the country; *The Rights of Gay People* (and similar publications on the rights of employees, Indians and tribes, women, and many other groups) ($2.50–$4.95); and works such as *The Hands That Feed Us: Undocumented Farm Workers in Florida* (1986, $5).

American Friends Service Committee (AFSC)
1501 Cherry Street
Philadelphia, PA 19102
(215) 241-7000
Asia A. Bennett, Executive Secretary

Founded in 1917 by American Quakers to provide conscientious objectors to war with a constructive alternative to military service, the AFSC today carries on a program of service, development, justice and peace under the direction of a Quaker Board and Corporation representing a wide spectrum of Quakers in America. Through its international headquarters in Philadelphia, its ten regional offices in the United States, and its program operations overseas, it works for the abolition of war and the fulfillment of human rights as essential twin goals to creating a nonviolent world in which all may live together. In the United States, the AFSC focuses on questions of exclusion and unequal opportunities in employment, education, administration of justice, land rights, welfare, and food programs.

PUBLICATIONS: Has an extensive publication program, including leaflets, pamphlets, newsletters, and books. Some of those on human rights subjects are *Breaking with a Bitter Past: Toward a New Relationship with Central America* (1987, free), *Lebanon: Toward Legal Order and Respect for Human Rights* (1983, $2), and *Listen Real Loud: News of Women's Liberation Worldwide* ($5–$10 sliding scale), a quarterly newsletter on national, international, and Third World feminist issues.

Americas Watch
36 West 44th Street
Suite 911 New York, NY 10036
(212) 840-9460
Aryeh Neier, Executive Director

1522 K Street, NW, Suite 910
Washington, DC 20005
(202) 371-6592
Juan Mendez, Director

The Americas Watch Committee, one of the three committees of Human Rights Watch, was established by the Fund for Free Expression in 1981 to monitor and promote observance of free expression and other internationally recognized human rights in Central America, South America, and the Caribbean. One of its original purposes was to counteract the approach to human rights espoused by some U.S. government officials who advocated a different approach to human rights abuses by "hostile totalitarian" governments as opposed to those by "friendly totalitarian" governments.

PUBLICATIONS: The committee has a prolific publication program, consisting mainly of reports of its fact-finding missions. Some are book-length (see the Monographs section in Chapter 5); others are briefer but of the same type. Among the more recent of these are the following: *A Certain Passivity: Failing To Curb Human Rights Abuses in Peru* (December 1987, $5), *Human Rights Concerns in Chile* (March 1987, $4), *Human Rights in Ecuador* (March 1988, $6), *Human Rights in Panama* (April 1988, $6), *Human Rights in Paraguay on the Eve of Elections* (December 1987, $3), *Police Abuses in Brazil* (December 1987, $5), *The Sumus in Nicaragua and Honduras: An Endangered People* (September 1987, $4), *Truth and Partial Justice in Argentina* (August 1987. $6), and

The Vicaria de la Solidaridad in Chile (December 1987, $4). It also publishes a periodic newsletter, *Chile News in Brief* ($20). A second newsletter, *Guatemala News in Brief,* ceased publication with issue no. 23 in 1988.

Amnesty International, USA (AIUSA)
322 Eighth Avenue
New York, NY 10001
(212) 807-8400
John G. Healy, Executive Director

Amnesty International is the largest human rights organization in the world. Like other sections around the world, AIUSA works impartially to (1) free prisoners of conscience (men, women, and children jailed solely for their beliefs, color, sex, ethnic origin, language, or religion, provided they have neither used nor advocated violence); (2) ensure fair trials for all political prisoners; and (3) abolish torture and executions. It works toward these goals through nationwide "adoption groups" that work for the release of prisoners of conscience, through its Urgent Action Network—letter-writing campaigns on behalf of persons in immediate danger—and other activities to raise the awareness of human rights violations. AIUSA is supported by research and program staff at its international headquarters in London.

PUBLICATIONS: Its extensive publications include full-length books (see the Monographs section in Chapter 5), an annual report on human rights in each country, many separate country reports, and special reports on topics such as the death penalty. Among its more recent reports are the following: *Afghanistan: Unlawful Killings and Torture* (1988, $2), *Bulgaria: Continuing Human Rights Abuses against Ethnic Turks* (1987, $3), *Burma: Extrajudicial Execution and Torture of Members of Ethnic Minorities* (1988, $5), *Chile: Briefing: "Disappearances"* (1988, $5), *China: Prisoners of Conscience in the People's Republic of China* (1987, $3), *Cuba: Recent Developments Affecting the Situation of Political Prisoners and the Use of the Death Penalty* (1988, $4), *El Salvador: "Death Squads"—A Government Strategy* (1988, $5), *Haiti: Deaths in Detention, Torture and Inhumane Prison Conditions* (1987, $4), *Iran: Violations of Human Rights* (1987, $6), *Morocco: Report on Torture* (1986, $3), *Nepal: A Pattern of Human Rights Violations* (1987, $3), *Nicaragua: The Human Rights Record* (1986, $5), *Panama: Assault on Human Rights* (1988, $3), *Philippines: Unlawful Killings by Military and Paramilitary Forces* (1988, $5), *Romania: Human Rights Violations in the Eighties* (1987, $4), *South Africa: An Amnesty International Briefing* (1986, $4), *Syria: Torture by Security Forces* (1987, $5), *United Kingdom: Alleged Forces Admissions during Incommunicado Detention* (1988, $4), *USA: The Death Penalty* (1987, $6), *USSR: Women Imprisoned in the "Small Zone"* (1985, $3), and *Zimbabwe: Memorandum to the Government* (1986, $3). AIUSA also publishes a bimonthly newsletter, *Amnesty Action,* for its members.

Anti-Defamation League of B'nai B'rith (ADL)
823 United Nations Plaza
New York, NY 10017
(212) 490-2525
Abraham H. Foxman, National Director

Dedicated to promoting understanding among peoples of different races, creeds, and ethnic backgrounds. In order to further interreligious understanding, the ADL has established relations with Christian institutions to help them create programs that reflect sensitivity and concern for the Jewish-Christian encounter. The ADL fights bigotry, discrimination, and anti-Semitism in all its forms; it attempts to protect the human rights of Jews throughout the world through its many programs.

PUBLICATIONS: Its comprehensive publication program includes reports, books, periodicals, and monographs focusing on topics such as prejudice, discrimination and intergroup relations, multicultural education, political and social issues, and the Holocaust. Its periodicals include *A Journal of Holocaust Studies* ($12), *Education and Society* ($18), and *Face to Face* ($12). Among its monographs appropriate to human rights topics are the following: *The Nature of Prejudice* ($8.95), *Racism and Sexism: Responding to the Challenge* ($8.75), *Anti-Semitism: A Case Study in Prejudice and Discrimination* ($2.50) and *Documents of the Holocaust* ($22.50).

Asia Coalition of Human Rights Organizations (ACHRO)
2713 Maria Aurora Street
Makati, Manila, Philippines
Dr. A. C. Esperitu, Contact Person

Founded in 1984 as an independent membership organization to help strengthen nongovernmental human rights organizations in Asia and enhance their capabilities for human rights activism. Some of its projects include research on freedom of association, implementation of a program on victim-group–oriented action research, and studies on the violations of the rights of support groups working with the rural poor.

PUBLICATIONS: Two of its publications are *Human Rights in Asia: Some Prospects, Problems, and Approaches* and *Human Rights Participatory Action Research: Some Case Studies.*

Asia Watch
36 West 44th Street, Suite 911
New York, NY 10036
(212) 840-9460
Eric Schwartz, Program Director

Established in 1985, Asia Watch attempts to respond to the important human rights struggles taking place in several countries of Asia. Similar to the other Watch Committees, it publicizes violations of human rights and launches international protests against governments that commit abuses. It frequently sends missions to countries where abuses are taking place, meeting with government officials, opposition leaders, local human rights groups, church officials, labor leaders, and others who can assist in providing accurate information.

PUBLICATIONS: In addition to book-length monographs (see the Monographs section in Chapter 5), Asia Watch publishes reports on fact-finding missions. Among the more recent are the following: *By All Parties to the Conflict: Violations of the Laws of War in Afghanistan* (March 1988, $8), *Human Rights in Tibet* (February 1988, $5), *Human Rights Concerns in Indonesia* (April 1986, $3), and *Still Confined: Journalists in "Re-Education" Camps and Prisons in Vietnam* (April 1987, $6).

Center for International Policy
236 Massachusetts Avenue, NE
Washington, DC 20002
(212) 544-4666
William Goodfellow, Director

Founded in 1975 as a project of the Fund for Peace, the Center for International Policy is a nonprofit education and research group concerned with U.S. policy towards the Third World and its impact on human rights and human needs. In the late 1970s, the Center persuaded the executive branch and Congress to extend human rights guidelines to many important but overlooked channels of U.S. aid. It carries out an extensive research and publication program on the implications of U.S. foreign aid, especially economic and military aid, to countries of Asia, Africa, and Latin America.

PUBLICATIONS: Its most important publication is the *International Policy Report* ($1.50–$2.00 per copy or $9 for a one-year subscription). It also issues the *Central America Negotiations Updates* ($10 per year; includes copies of any *International Policy Report* dealing with the topic) and a *Newsletter*. Some of its more recent *Reports* are the following: *Compliance: The Central American Peace Accord* (November 1987, $1.50), *Arias Primer* (June 1987, $1.50), and *Destabilizing Angola: South Africa's War and U.S. Policy* (December 1986, $2). An earlier three-part series specifically on human rights includes *The Financial Hit List* (1984), *Human Rights: The Carter Record; the Reagan Reaction* (1984), and *Enforcing Human Rights: Congress and the Multilateral Banks* (1985, $1.50 each).

Center for the Study of Human Rights
704 International Affairs Building
Columbia University
420 West 118th Street
New York, NY 10027
(212) 280-2479

Dr. J. Paul Martin, Executive Director

Established at Columbia University in 1977 to promote teaching and research on human rights in national and international contexts. The Center's activities involve all disciplines and address both theoretical and policy questions. An integral part of the University, the Center benefits extensively from Columbia University faculty and resources. Each year the Center sponsors a Human Rights Research and Teaching Symposium and also offers a fellowship to a student working on a Ph.D. dissertation related to human rights.

PUBLICATIONS: The Center publishes occasional scholarly papers, a periodic newsletter, and syllabi for graduate and undergraduate instruction in human rights. It sponsored *Human Rights: A Topical Bibliography* (See the Reference Materials section in Chapter 5) and *Human Rights in Contemporary China* (see the Monographs section in Chapter 5).

Chile Information Network
Box 20179
Cathedral Finance Station
New York, NY 10025
Rev. David L. Maxwell, Coordinator

A nationwide network of academics, religious and social activists, community leaders, and others working for human rights in Chile. Under the sponsorship of the Chile Center for Education and Development at the same address, it is concerned with such issues as disappearances, working and health conditions, and women's rights. Publishes *Chile Net,* a newsletter on human rights conditions in Chile and the activities of network members.

Clergy and Laity Concerned (CALC)
198 Broadway, Room 302
New York, NY 10038
(212) 964-6730
Sheila Collins, Co-Director

An interfaith and multiracial network of 57 chapters and action groups in 31 states working primarily through the religious community for justice and peace. Its human rights program focuses on human rights violations in countries where U.S. and U.S.-based multinational corporations and banks are prominent. It organizes to stop U.S. support for regimes that deny basic political and social rights.

PUBLICATIONS: *CALC Report* (6 issues per year; free to members) is the official publication of CALC. It examines issues of concern to the organization in interviews, analyses, scriptural reflections, and action handles. Recent issues have been devoted to such topics as South Africa, Native Americans, and intervention in the Third World.

Coalition for a New Foreign Policy
712 G Street
Washington, DC 20003
(202) 546-8400
David Reed, Director

A coalition of many civic, religious, peace, and public interest groups founded in 1976 to influence Congress and the administration to develop a more humanitarian foreign policy. Many of its activities are related to human rights issues, particularly those focusing on Africa and Central America. It also sponsors Interfaith Advocacy Training Workshops.

PUBLICATIONS: It issues occasional Action Alerts and Action Guides in addition to its quarterly newsletter, *Coalition Close Up.*

Commission for the Defense of Human Rights in Central America
Apportado Postal 189
Paseo de las Estudiantes
San José, Costa Rica
213462-33 3326
Isolda Arita, General Coordinator

Founded in 1978 to promote and defend human rights in Central America. Coordinates and supports the national nongovernmental human rights organizations within their respective countries. Some of its activities include human rights education, following up on allegations of human rights violations, legal assistance, and coordinating a regional information network.

PUBLICATIONS: Its publications include a monthly bulletin on the human rights situation in Central America (*Documentacion sobre Derechos Humanos*), occasional papers and reports, and monthly bibliographies on human rights.

Cultural Survival, Inc.
11 Divinity Avenue
Cambridge, MA 02138
(617) 495-2562
Jason Clay, Director of Research

Founded in 1972 for the purpose of helping indigenous people survive and adapt to the world around them. Made up of indigenous people, ethnic minorities, academics interested in the Third World, research institutes and museums, government agencies, and other interested individuals, Cultural Survival sponsors projects designed to promote human rights for indigenous people and help them become successful ethnic minorities. Maintains a library and speakers' bureau and also conducts seminars and research on problems confronting indigenous peoples.

PUBLICATIONS: In addition to its annual report and occasional special reports, it publishes the *Cultural Survival Quarterly* and *Cultural Survival Reports.*

Fund for Free Expression
36 West 44th Street, Suite 9ll
New York, NY 10036
(212) 840-9460
Sophie C. Silberberg, Executive Director

Organized in 1975 to aid the worldwide struggle by authors, journalists, and all others to speak and publish without fear of reprisal. Its defense of free expression is based on Article 19 of the Universal Declaration of Human Rights. The fund sponsors many educational and public policy projects. Out of its concern for human rights in general came the Watch Committees—Americas Watch, Asia Watch, and Helsinki Watch.

PUBLICATIONS: The fund publishes reports on freedom of expression in various parts of the world and sponsors journals and newsletters abroad. The one best known in the United States is the British publication *Index on Censorship.* Reports include *Intellectual Freedom in China—An Update* (1985, $5) and *Israeli Censorship of Arab Publications* (1984, $10).

Fund for Open Information and Accountability, Inc. (FOIA)
145 West 4th Street
New York, NY 10012
(212) 477-3188
Ann Mari Buitrago, Director

Organized in 1977 to defend, strengthen, and accomplish the purpose of the Freedom of Information Act, FOIA is particularly interested in issues of government secrecy. It works in conjunction with a network of national and grassroots organizations in protecting the public's right to know and in exposing government misconduct in this area. It assists individuals and organizations with the procedures involved in obtaining information through the Freedom of Information Act.

PUBLICATIONS: Its principal publication is *Our Right To Know* ($10), a quarterly that contains articles, news items, and "FOIA in the Courts." It also publishes occasional fact sheets and legislative alerts.

Guatemala Human Rights Commission/USA
1359 Monroe Street, NE
Washington, DC 20017
(202) 529-6599
Alice Zachmann, SSND, Coordinator

A private, nonprofit organization that seeks to raise the awareness of people in the United States regarding human rights violations in Guatemala, and specifically to urge the release of "disappeared" or detained Guatemalans and to work for the improvement of human rights in Guatemala. Encourages members to become Advocates who respond to Human Rights Alerts that document specific cases of human rights violations and who help to provide assistance to victims of these violations.

PUBLICATIONS: Its bimonthly *Information Bulletin* ($10) contains articles and detailed accounts, with names and dates, of violations of human rights.

Helsinki Watch
36 West 44th Street
New York, NY 10036
(212) 840-9460
Jeri Laber, Executive Director

Established in 1979 in response to the persecution of citizens in the Soviet Union and Czechoslovakia for their attempts to organize groups to monitor compliance to the Helsinki accords in those countries. While concerned with human rights practices in each of the 35 Helsinki countries, Helsinki Watch has centered its efforts on the more egregious offenders—namely, the Warsaw Pact countries and Turkey and Yugoslavia. It has also monitored human rights abuses in Afghanistan because many of these have been committed directly by a Helsinki signatory, the Soviet Union. It was the first of the Watch committees that are now collectively called Human Rights Watch.

PUBLICATIONS: In addition to a number of book-length publications (see the Monographs section in Chapter 5), Helsinki Watch has published many reports of its fact-finding missions. Among the more recent are the following: *By All Parties to the Conflict: Violations of the Laws of War in Afghanistan* (March 1988, $8); *Destroying Ethnic Identity: The Kurds of Turkey* (March 1988, $6); *Destroying Ethnic Identity: The Turks of Bulgaria— An Update* (September 1987, $5); *The Moscow Helsinki Monitors: Their Vision, Their Achievement, the Price They Paid* (May 1986, $5); *Mothers of Exiles: Refugees Imprisoned in America* (June 1986, $8); and a series, *Violations of the Helsinki Accords* in Bulgaria, Czechoslovakia, East Germany, Poland, Romania, Turkey, the USSR, and Yugoslavia (1986–1987, $5–$8).

Honduras Information Center
One Summer Street
Somerville, MA 02143
(617) 522-6240

An organization founded in 1982 by Hondurans and Americans concerned about the effects of U.S. policy in Central America, particularly in Honduras. The center collects information from various organizations in Honduras, e.g., the human rights and refugee organizations, and also from sources in the United States and makes it available through its newsletter. It maintains files on human rights abuses and on the media in Honduras.

PUBLICATION: *Honduras Update*, a monthly ($22; individuals, $14).

Human Rights Advocates International (HRAI)
230 Park Avenue, Suite 460
New York, NY 10169
(212) 986-5555
Charles F. Printz, Executive Director

Lawyers, scholars, and others interested in constitutional law and human rights founded HRAI in 1979 to foster human rights through providing legal services, counseling, and investigating human rights abuses. HRAI also conducts research and offers seminars on human rights law. Its members act as representatives for exiles, member states of the U.N., individual citizens, and the Amerasian children of Vietnam veterans.

PUBLICATIONS: HRAI is responsible for editing *Constitutions of the Countries of the World* and *Constitutions of Dependencies and Special Sovereignties*. It also publishes reports on its research.

Human Rights Internet (HRI)
Harvard Law School
Pound Hall, Room 401
Cambridge, MA 02138
(617) 495-4536
Laurie S. Wiseberg, Executive Director

HRI furthers the defense of human rights through the dissemination of information. It is an international communications network and clearinghouse on human rights with universal coverage. Over 2,000 organizations and individuals contribute to the network. It also actively promotes teaching and research on human rights. Its publications and services are undoubtedly the most useful of any available to those seriously working for the promotion of human rights. It not only has its own extensive publication program, but it maintains a documentation center rich in the publications of other human rights organizations.

PUBLICATIONS: HRI publishes the single most important journal publication in the field—the *Human Rights Internet Reporter* (see the Periodicals section in Chapter 5) and also a series of human rights directories (see the Reference Materials section in Chapter 5). In addition to these, it has published *Teaching Human Rights* (1981, $20) and

Access to Justice: The Struggle for Human Rights in South East Asia (1985, $10.25). It has also made available on microfiche a substantial part of its documentary collection of nongovernmental human rights organizations materials.

Human Rights Watch
36 West 44th Street
New York, NY 10036
(212) 840-9460
Aryeh Neier, Executive Director

An organization that links the Watch Committees—Helsinki Watch, Americas Watch, and Asia Watch—and is responsible for forming new Watch Committees in other parts of the world. Its activities are governed by the boards of the three Watch Committees and the board of the organization from which the Watch Committees grew—the Fund for Free Expression, established in 1975. Human Rights Watch monitors the human rights practices of governments: murders, disappearances, kidnappings, torture, imprisonment for nonviolent expression or association, exile, psychiatric abuse, censorship, and deprivations of political freedom. It works through the three Committees but occasionally undertakes special projects in regions not covered by the Watch Committees. In addition to monitoring abuses, it launches international protests against governments that commit abuses and encourages professionals and special interest groups to do likewise.

PUBLICATIONS: Its publication program is carried on through the three Watch Committees for the most part, but it does publish more general works, sometimes with the Lawyers Committee for Human Rights. Typical of these are *The Persecution of Human Rights Monitors: December 1986 to December 1987, A Worldwide Survey* (December 1987, $7); *Four Failures: A Report on the U.N. Special Rapporteurs on Human Rights in Chile, Guatemala, Iran, and Poland* (January 1986, $4); and *Critique of the Department of State's Country Reports on Human Rights Practices for 1987* (June 1988, $12).

Humanitas International Human Rights Committee
P.O. Box 818
Menlo Park, CA 94206
(415) 324-9077
Ed Lazer, Associate Director

An independent nonprofit organization founded by Joan Baez in 1979 to work for human rights, nonviolence, and disarmament. The committee conducts educational and advocacy programs on human rights issues, assists in nonviolent conflict resolution, and provides help to political refugees. It also conducts seminars and workshops on peace and human rights issues.

PUBLICATION: *Humanitas Newsletter,* a quarterly.

Institute for Policy Studies
1601 Connecticut Avenue, NW
Washington, DC 20009
(202) 234-9382
Diana Vegh, Executive Director

Founded in 1963 as a transnational center for research, education, and social invention. The institute critically examines the assumptions and policies that define American posture on domestic and international issues and offers alternative strategies and visions. One of its areas of concern is human rights. In memory of Orlando Letelier and Ronni Karpen-Moffitt, both strong human rights advocates who were assassinated, the Institute established the Letelier-Moffitt Fund for Human Rights, which is designed to explore human rights issues, especially those involving the relation between economic policy and the denial of human rights.

PUBLICATIONS: Publishes books, occasional reports, and policy papers. Two of its recent books are *Nicaragua: The Price of Intervention* (1988, $8.95) and *In Whose Interest: A Guide to U.S.–South Africa Relations* (1985, $11.95).

Institute for the Study of Genocide (ISG)
445 West 56th Street, Room 3114S
New York, NY 10019
(212) 489-3697
Helen Fein, Ph.D., Executive Director

The institute, a nonprofit educational organization, was founded in 1982 to promote teaching and scholarship on the causes, consequences, and prevention of genocide. It supports scholars from various disciplines in the conduct of their research, in the publication of their findings, and in the application of these findings to classroom teaching. It uses the resources and facilities of the John Jay College of Criminal Justice and also maintains its own library of resources pertaining to genocide.

PUBLICATIONS: Publishes *The ISG Newsletter* and occasional pamphlets on current issues relating to genocide.

Inter-American Commission on Human Rights (IACHR). See Organization of American States (OAS).

Intercommunity Center for Justice and Peace
20 Washington Square North
New York, NY 10011
(212) 475-6677

Darlene Cuccinello, Coordinator of Human Rights

A coalition of 41 Catholic religious orders in the Tri-State area of New York, New Jersey, and Connecticut that seek to assist victims of injustice by trying to change the structures that cause violations of human rights. The focus of the center's human rights work is Central America. It seeks dialogue with interfaith communities, universities, and other groups about U.S. foreign policy and the militarization of Central America. It also aids refugees from that region.

PUBLICATION: *Annual Report.*

International Association against Torture (AICT)
New York Section
AICT NGO Office
P.O. Box 1752
Cathedral Station
New York, NY 10025
(212) 928-7600
Rev. David Kalke, Coordinator

An international human rights organization founded in 1977 in Italy to promote the dignity of individuals and end the practice of torture, particularly in Latin America and the Caribbean. Its goals are to denounce torture and other types of human rights violations, to struggle against such practices, and to organize solidarity with those who are suffering or have suffered previously because of these violations. To denounce crimes against the rights of people, it uses all possible means of sharing information, including documentation centers, conferences, painting and film expositions, fact-finding delegations, reports, public demonstrations, and concrete actions of solidarity with victims of torture. It holds Non-Governmental Organization (NGO) Category II status at the U.N., which enables it, through oral statements and written documents and reports, to draw attention to the human rights situations in the Latin American countries needing the attention of the U.N.

PUBLICATIONS: Occasional reports on the human rights situation in a particular country of Latin America or the Caribbean. Two 1988 reports available for $5 from the U.S. Office are on Cuba and El Salvador.

International Association of Official Human Rights Agencies (IAOHRA)
444 North Capitol Street, Suite 249
Washington, DC 20001
(202) 624-5410
Ernest Pete Ward, Executive Director

Established for governmental human rights agencies in 1949 for the purpose of fostering better human relations and enhancing human rights under the law. IAOHRA has offered extensive services and training for personnel of state and local human rights agencies throughout the United States. It conducts workshops and seminars for human rights administrators and has established an electronic clearinghouse for information exchange and technical updates. It also promotes development of state legislation through its technical assistance workshops for state and regional planning agencies.

PUBLICATIONS: Its principal publications are the *IAOHRA News*, a quarterly, and periodic *Technical Notes*.

International Human Rights Law Group
733 15th Street, NW, Suite 1000
Washington, DC 20005
(202) 639-8016
Amy Young, Executive Director

Established in 1978 as a nonprofit public interest law center concerned with the promotion and protection of international human rights. The Law Group provides information and legal assistance to organizations and individuals in cases of human rights violations. Funded by foundation grants and individual contributions and assisted in its work by attorneys in Washington, D.C., the Law Group offers its expertise on a *pro bono* basis.

PUBLICATIONS: The Group has an extensive publication program. It sponsors some full-length books, e.g., Hannum's *Guide to Human Rights Practice* (see the Monographs section in Chapter 5) and a newsletter, *The Law Group Docket* ($20). It also publishes a Legal Studies Series. Among the works in this series are *Legal Treatment of Koreans in Japan: The Impact of International Human Rights Law on Japanese Law* (1986, $7), *Waiting for Justice: Treatment of Political Prisoners under El Salvador's Decree 50* (1987, $7), and *Government Restrictions on the Press in South Africa: The State of Emergency and International Law* (1987, $6). Another set of publications is its Election Observer Series. Some of the titles in this series are *Report on the Chilean Electoral Process* (1987, $5), *Political Transition and the Rule of Law in Guatemala* (1987, $5), and *The 1987 Korean Presidential Election* (1988, $5).

International Justice Network (IJN)
3029 Fourth Street, NE
Washington, DC 20017
(202) 832-3112
Adela Gross, OSF, Liaison

An affiliate organization of the U.S. Catholic Mission Association, IJN is a coalition of religious groups interested in peace and justice issues. Its purpose is to be a conduit for the voice of Third World peoples in their struggle for human rights and justice. Network members gather information from Third World contacts, analyze it, and facilitate a corporate response from U.S. religious groups.

International League for Human Rights
432 Park Avenue South, Room 1103
New York, NY 10016
(213) 684-1221
Felice D. Gaer, Executive Director

Tracing its roots to a citizens' league in France in the early 1900s, the International League for Human Rights today provides advice, resources, and publicity to affiliated human rights groups throughout the world. Through its Defenders' Project, the league energetically seeks to protect courageous advocates of human rights in repressive societies. Among its activities are the reunification of families, assisting victims of discrimination, sending special investigative missions to regions where human rights violations occur, negotiating with repressive governments to obtain relief for human rights victims, and sending observers to political trials.

PUBLICATIONS: The league has an extensive publication program. In addition to its periodic *Human Rights Bulletin* (free to members) and *Annual Report*, it issues many reports on human rights in various regions of the world. Some of these are *Human Rights in Poland* (1987, $6), *Human Rights in Czechoslovakia* (1987, $8), *Human Rights in Palau: Report of an Observer Mission* (1987, $10), *Human Rights in Zaire* (1987, $6), *Tunisia's Human Rights Record* (1986, $5), *Workers' Rights in South Korea* (1987, $5), and *The U.N. Financial Crisis and Its Potential Effects on Human Rights* (1986, $2.50).

Lawyers Committee for Human Rights
330 Seventh Avenue, 10th Floor
New York, NY 10001
(212) 629-6170
Michael Posner, Executive Director

The Lawyers Committee was founded in 1978 to protect and promote the most basic and fundamental rights of the individual. In the best tradition of the law profession, the committee gathers facts and demands explanations on behalf of victims of human rights abuses abroad and of refugees seeking political asylum in the United States. Through its International Human Rights Program, the committee has investigated patterns of abuse in Asia, Africa, the Middle East, Eastern Europe and the Soviet Union, and Latin America and the Caribbean. Its detailed and carefully researched reports, occasionally published in cooperation with one of the Human Rights Watch Committees, are often used by diplomats, policymakers, the media, and others in the United States and abroad.

PUBLICATIONS: The committee has published many reports of its fact-finding missions in addition to reports on U.S. human rights policy and asylum training materials (see the Monographs section in Chapter 5 for recent book-length publications). Some of the more recent reports are *From the Ashes: Justice in El Salvador* (1987, $8), *Deaths in Custody: Seven Recent Cases in South Africa* (1986, $6), *Zimbabwe: Wages of War* (1986, $10), *Human Rights in Nicaragua: 1987* (1987, $5), and *Vigilante Violence: A Report on Human Rights in the Philippines* (1988, $10).

Meiklejohn Civil Liberties Institute
P.O. Box 673
Berkeley, CA 94701
(415) 848-0599
Ann Fagan Ginger, President

Has been described as "a grassroots legal thinktank for peace and human rights." The institute was founded in 1965 as an archives for attorney workpapers and court papers filed in civil rights cases, to assist lawyers and others working for civil and human rights causes. It is particularly concerned with peace law, which it believes grew out of the universal demand after World War II for an end to war as a method of settling international disputes and for the formulation of procedures to stop the use of force; peace law includes legislation passed by governmental bodies from local to global.

PUBLICATIONS: *The Peace Law Docket 1946–1988,* still in preparation, documents cases of people arrested in demonstrations and people suing the government and weapons manufacturers for damages, mostly in state or federal courts but some in the World Court. Other publications are *News from MCLI,* issued semiannually; *Human Rights Organizations and Periodicals Directory* (see the Reference Materials section in Chapter 5); and *The Cold War against Labor* (1987, $39.95; $19.95, paper).

Minority Rights Group (MRG)
35 Claremont Avenue, Apartment 4S
New York, NY 10027
(212) 864-7986
Sue Roff, Convenor

The Minority Rights Group is an international research and information group registered in Britain as an educational trust. It is devoted to reducing the violations of human rights in all countries and to securing justice for minority (or majority) groups suffering discrimination. From its headquarters in London and chapters in ten countries throughout the world, the MRG continuously surveys current events to monitor situations globally. It aims to maintain an international balance, to remain politically impartial, and to address some lesser-known instances as well as more publicized cases of discrimination.

PUBLICATIONS: Its reports are vital background papers that cover many subjects with wide-ranging political implications, such as female circumcision, Europe's migrant workers, and the untouchables of India. Each report is approximately 20 pages, includes an exhaustive bibliography, and is usually illustrated with maps, charts, and other statistical evidence. Some of its recent reports are *Haitian Refugees in the U.S.,* *Minorities and Human Rights Law,* and *Roma: Europe's Gypsies* (1987, $3.95 each or six reports for $20). The headquarters in London also issues a newsletter, *Outsider,* available to members who pay $5 a year.

National Center for Policy Alternatives
200 Florida Avenue, NW
Fourth Floor, Room 412
Washington, DC 20009
(202) 387-6030
Linda Tarr-Whelan, President/Executive Director

Founded in 1975 as a progressive nonpartisan, nonprofit public policy center focusing on innovation at the state and local levels. Provides policymakers with field-based services, national resources, and connections to advocates and experts. Serves as a catalyst for innovative public policy. Although its primary focus is on state and local policy, some of its program areas are human rights issues: family and work, women's rights, housing, and environmental security.

PUBLICATIONS: Its quarterly newsletter, *Ways and Means* ($15), emphasizes new approaches to state and local government problems. Two of its publications on human rights issues are *The Women's Economic Justice Agenda* (1987, $12.95) and *Winning the Right to Know: A Handbook for Toxic Activists* (1983, $8.95).

New York CIRCUS
P.O. Box 37
Times Square Station
New York, NY 10108
(212) 928-7600
David Kalke, Executive Director

An ecumenical collective founded in 1975 that grew out of the specialized ministries program of the Metropolitan New York Synod of the Lutheran Church in America. It joins with other Christians who participate in the struggle for justice and liberation, with a primary focus on the popular church in Latin America. In order to pursue its goals, it operates a research, documentation, and action center for social justice and international awareness.

PUBLICATIONS: Include *New York CIRCUS Ink*, an occasional newsletter, and *Lucha Struggle*, a bimonthly journal of Christian reflection on struggles for liberation ($10, individuals; $20, institutions).

Organization of American States (OAS)
Inter-American Commission on Human Rights (IACHR)
General Secretariat
Washington, DC 20006
(202) 458-6002
Edmundo Vargas, Executive Secretary

The OAS is an international organization created by the American States to achieve an order of peace and justice, to promote and defend solidarity, territorial integrity, and independence. The IACHR was created as part of a resolution adopted in Santiago, Chile, in 1959 and was more clearly defined at an OAS meeting in La Paz, Bolivia, in 1979 as "an organization of the OAS, created to promote the observance and defense of human rights and to serve as a consultative organ of the Organization in this matter." Human rights are understood to be those set forth in the American Convention, "Human Rights and the American Declaration of the Rights and Duties of Man."

PUBLICATIONS: Among the numerous publications of the OAS, many in Spanish, are the following: *Basic Documents Pertaining to Human Rights in the Inter-American System* (1988, $10), Reports on the situation of human rights in member countries ($3–$12), *Human Rights in the Americas* (1984, $17.50), and a quarterly *Legal Newsletter* ($12).

Palestine Human Rights Campaign (PHRC)
220 South State Street, #1308
Chicago, IL 60604
(312) 987-1830
Rev. Donald E. Wagner, National Director

Founded in 1977 to defend the rights of Palestinians living in the occupied territories. The PHRC seeks to defend the human rights of Palestinians as these rights are defined in the Universal Declaration of Human Rights. It investigates violations and makes them public in order to raise people's awareness regarding the plight of the Palestinians. It does this through seminars, publications, and lectures.

PUBLICATIONS: It publishes the bimonthly *Palestine Human Rights Newsletter* and occasional reports on human rights abuses. The PHRC Database Program Monthly Update is also available ($50 per year).

PEN American Center
568 Broadway
New York, NY 10012
(212) 334-1660
Karen Kennerly, Director

The American branch of International PEN (Poets, Playwrights, Essayists, Editors, and Novelists), which also includes historians, critics, journalists, and translators. PEN was founded in 1921 and has approximately 90 centers throughout the world. Its purpose is to protect the principles of unhampered transmission of free thought and to preserve the concept of a free press, within each nation and among all nations. Members pledge themselves to vigorously oppose any suppression of freedom of expression in the community to which they belong.

PUBLICATIONS: *Liberty Denied* (1988, $6.95) and the *PEN Newsletter* ($5).

Physicians for Human Rights (PHR)
408 Highland Avenue
Somerville, MA 02144
(617) 623-1930
Jonathan Fine, M.D., Executive Director

PHR is a national organization of health professionals founded in 1986 to bring the skills and influence of the medical community to the support of international human rights. It works to prevent the participation of doctors in torture, to defend imprisoned health professionals, to stop physical and psychological abuse of citizens by their governments, and to provide medical and humanitarian aid to victims of repression.

PUBLICATIONS: PHR has an extensive publication program. Members receive the *Physicians for Human Rights RECORD* four times a year and *Medical Action Alerts* requesting letters to be sent on behalf of specific victims of abuse. It also publishes very thorough reports of fact-finding missions. Three of the most recent are *The Casualties of Conflict: Medical Care and Human Rights in the West Bank and Gaza Strip* (March 1988, $4), *Panama 1987: Health Consequences of Police and Military Actions* (April 1988, $6), and *Sowing Fear: The Uses of Torture and Psychological Abuse in Chile* (October 1988, $7).

Survival International, U.S.A. (SIUSA)
2121 Decatur Place, NW
Washington, DC 20008
(202) 265-1077
Kenneth I. Taylor, Executive Director

A nonprofit human rights organization founded in 1979 to work for the rights of indigenous peoples around the world in their struggle to survive and determine their own futures without harmful outside interference. SIUSA attempts to raise the awareness of the public and particularly of legislators regarding human rights viololations against indigenous peoples. A group that sponsors research and educational activities, SIUSA is the U.S. National Section of the worldwide Survival International, which has its secretariat in London.

PUBLICATIONS: *Survival International News* is published by the London staff but distributed to all members. It also makes available its reports and other types of documents. The U.S. section publishes *Notes from SIUSA* and periodic reports, such as *Counter-Insurgency and Tribal Peoples in the Philippines* (1988, $3).

Third World Resources
464 Nineteenth Street
Oakland, CA 94612
(415) 835-4692
Tom Fenton and Mary Heffron, Directors

Third World Resources, a financially independent affiliate of the Data Center at the same address, is a documentation clearinghouse and computer-accessible databank on Third World–related organizations and materials. It makes these materials accessible through its many publications, most of which contain a great deal of human rights–related information.

PUBLICATIONS: These include the quarterly *Third World Resources* ($25 per year; individuals, $25 for two years). Each issue includes organizations, books, periodicals, articles, pamphlets, and audiovisual materials. It also publishes very useful directories. Some of these are *Middle East: A Directory of Resources* (1988, $9.95), *Africa: A Directory of Resources* (1988, $9.95), and *Women in the Third World: A Directory of Resources* (1987, $9.95).

United Nations Centre for Human Rights
8-14 avenue de la Paix
1211 Geneva 10, Switzerland

Although the U.N. General Assembly and several of its subsidiary bodies deal with human rights, since 1946 the Commission on Human Rights has been the main body charged with the task of preserving and promoting human rights. The commission makes studies, prepares recommendations, and drafts international instruments relating to human rights. It has established a number of subsidiary bodies to assist in this work, e.g. the Sub-Committee on the Prevention of Discrimination and Protection of Minorities and the Working Group on Enforced or Involuntary Disappearances. These various groups meet with governments to discuss alleged violations of human rights and, when sufficiently serious, may launch an investigation by experts in order to initiate a dialogue with the government to bring about change.

PUBLICATIONS: The U.N. has a very extensive publication program in many areas—human rights being one. Most of these are available in the United States from the New York office: Center for Human Rights, United Nations, New York, NY 10017. Some of the publications available free in single copies are *Human Rights: Questions and Answers* (June, 1988), *Human Rights Machinery* (December 1987), and *The International Bill of Rights* (April 1988). Others include *Food as a Human Right* (1985, $12), *Exploitation of Labor through Illicit and Clandestine Trafficking* (1986, $17.50), and *Conscientious Objection in Military Service* (1986, $6).

U.S. Department of State
Office of Human Rights
Bureau of Human Rights and Humanitarian Affairs
Washington, DC 20520
Richard W. Aherne, Director

The bureau has primary responsibility for the development and implementation of U.S. human rights policy. The criteria or broad standards used in assessing any country's human rights performance are integrity of the individual, civil rights, and political rights. The bureau draws upon the reports of the U.N., human rights groups, information provided by human rights officers in U.S. embassies, and the Universal Declaration of Human Rights for standards, information, and analysis of a country's performance.

PUBLICATIONS: Each year the bureau compiles and presents to Congress *Country Reports on Human Rights Practices* (see the Monographs section in Chapter 5). It also publishes transcripts of speeches on human rights given by various Department of State personnel; these are part of the Current Policy series distributed by the Bureau of Public Affairs. Two examples from this series are *U.S. Human Rights Policy: An Overview* (June 1988) and *Human Rights and U.S. Foreign Policy* (May 1987).

World Policy Institute
777 United Nations Plaza
New York, NY 10017
(212) 490-1482
Archibald L. Gillies, President

Founded in 1948, the World Policy Institute is a not-for-profit educational organization that, though focusing on the U.S. political debate, emphasizes the development of world policies—initiatives that reflect the stake the United States has in common security and development with other nations. The institute is concerned with basic human rights issues such as peace and global security, human development, and the right of all peoples to self-determination.

PUBLICATIONS: The institute's primary publication is the *World Policy Journal* ($20, individuals; $26, institutions), a quarterly devoted to the discussion of U.S. foreign policy and international economic and security questions. It also publishes reports such as *Looking toward '88: The Politics of American Identity* (1987, $3) and *Defining American Strength* (1987, $3) and occasional curriculum materials such as *World Military and Social Expenditures, 1987–1988* (1988, $6).

5

Books and Periodicals

Reference Materials

The following, except for the indexing and abstracting publications, are reference tools emphasizing human rights. The bibliographies are particularly helpful in locating earlier materials. Many general reference tools can also be helpful in locating useful material on the subject.

Bibliographies and Guides

Andrews, J. A., and W. D. Hines. **Keyguide to Information Sources on the International Protection of Human Rights.** New York: Facts on File, 1987. 169p. $40. ISBN 0-8160-1822-7. K3236 A53.

Originally published in Great Britain, this guide provides a bibliography of basic materials on human rights, particularly from a legal and comparative standpoint. It includes an introduction to the concept of human rights, sections on the international and regional instruments for the protection of human rights, annotated lists of books and journals, and information on inter-and nongovernmental agencies. Emphasis is on British sources, but most basic North American works are also included.

Columbia University Center for the Study of Human Rights. **Human Rights: A Topical Bibliography.** Boulder, CO: Westview Press, 1983. 299p. $29.50. ISBN 0-86531-571-X. Z7164 L6 H84.

Prepared by the staff at the Center for the Study of Human Rights, this bibliography includes more than 7,000 scholarly books and articles drawn primarily from law, philosophy, and the social sciences. Limited to works in English published through 1981, the entries are arranged in a detailed classification scheme with an author index. Includes reference sources and selected periodicals and organizations.

Downing, Theodore E., and Gilbert Kushner, eds., with Human Rights Internet. **Anthropology and Human Rights** (Cultural Survival Report 24). Cambridge, MA: Cultural Survival, 1987. 250p. $10. ISBN 0-939521-29-6.

Though not a reference book in the strict sense of the word, this volume is included because its second half contains the most extensive bibliography on anthropology and human rights available. Originally prepared by Human Rights Internet with a grant from UNESCO, the work contains nearly 1,000 entries divided into such categories as Racism, Apartheid, Indigenous Rights, Genocide and Ethnocide, Torture, and Rights of the Child.

Friedman, Julian, and Marc I. Sherman, eds. **Human Rights: An International and Comparative Law Bibliography.** Westport, CT: Greenwood Press, 1985. 867p. $75. ISBN 0-313-24767-6. K3236 H86.

Drawing on materials in over 20 languages, this comprehensive bibliography presents more than 4,000 citations of primary and secondary sources on international and comparative human rights law. Cross-cultural, and to some extent interdisciplinary, the work is arranged in two main sections—the first on rights, the second on institutions—with a third section listing sources used in preparing the volume. Contains an author and secondary subject index.

Gelman, Anne, and Milos Stehlik. **Human Rights Film Guide.** Chicago, IL: Facets Multimedia, 1985. JC571 G42.

A descriptive guide to over 400 films and videotapes on human rights, covering such topics as imprisonment and torture, civil and political rights, refugees, labor rights, the death penalty, and freedom of expression and assembly. Films are arranged by broad subject categories but indexed by title and by country depicted. Each film is annotated and information on the type of media, producer, length, language, date, and distributor is given.

Library of Congress. Hispanic Division. **Human Rights in Latin America, 1964–1980.** Washington, DC: Library of Congress, 1983. 257p. ISBN 0-8444-0415-2. Z7164 L6 H85.

This is a selected bibliography of 1,827 annotated citations drawn from international law, theology, political theory, political economy, political science, history, and literature. Based on the collection at the Library of Congress, the work is arranged by country and issuing agency with an author index. Appendix includes a list of human rights organizations.

Miller, William, ed. **International Human Rights: A Bibliography, 1970–1976.** Notre Dame, IN: Center for Civil Rights, University of Notre Dame, 1976. 118p. K3236 M54.

This annotated bibliography of over 1,000 articles on human rights draws for the most part from standard journals and collected volumes on human rights. Arranged by author with a subject index.

Stanek, Edward. **A Bibliography of Selected Human Rights Bibliographies, Documentary Compilations, Periodicals, Reports and Reference Books Essential for the Study of International and Comparative Law of Human Rights** (Public Administration Series, Bibliography #P 2191). Monticello, IL: Vance Bibliographies, 1987. 12p. $3.75. ISBN 1-55590-371-1. Z7164 A2 P7.

This volume presents basic sources on human rights with some emphasis on Canadian works; it includes major human rights periodicals, yearbooks and reports, and selected directories, handbooks, manuals, and dictionaries. Monographs are arranged by author or issuing agency; periodicals, by title.

Directories

Christiano, David, and Lisa Young, eds. **Human Rights Organizations and Periodicals Directory.** 5th ed. Berkeley: Meiklejohn Civil Liberties Institute. 1983. 247p. $22. ISSN 0098-0579. KF4741 H84.

This guide includes nearly 700 groups, periodicals and other sources for teachers, students, and researchers seeking information on improving human rights in the United States. Though somewhat out of date, the work serves as a referral list for activists and others needing information or assistance on issues and problems affecting the public welfare. In addition to the main alphabetical list, there are a Federal Agencies Guide, a Subject Index, a Periodicals Index, and a Geographic Index.

Garling, Marguerite. **The Human Rights Handbook: A Guide to British and American International Human Rights Organizations.** Compiled for Writers and Scholars Educational Trust. New York: Facts on File, 1979. 299p. ISBN 0-87196-403-1. JC571 G184h.

Although somewhat out of date, this handbook provides basic background information on human rights organizations arranged by British,

North American, nongovernmental international groups, and intergovernmental international groups, within each of these by type of organization, and finally by specific groups such as journalists or lawyers. Information for each includes goals, structure, financing, and services to members.

Wiseberg, Laurie S., ed. **Human Rights Internet Directory: Eastern Europe and the USSR.** Cambridge, MA: Human Rights Internet, 1987. 304p. $30. ISBN 0-939338-03-3. JC599 E92H86.

The fourth in the Human Rights Internet (HRI) directory series, this volume, covering the Soviet Union and East European countries, has three component elements: (1) over 225 East European and Soviet "unofficial" organizations, groups, and publications that have emerged from the region since the early 1970s; (2) a number of "approved" human rights organizations based in Eastern Europe; and (3) organizations outside the region that monitor human rights activities. Arranged by country with indexes to organizations, individual names, and serial publications.

Wiseberg, Laurie S., and Harry M. Scoble, eds. **Human Rights Directory: Latin America, Africa, Asia.** Washington, DC: Human Rights Internet, 1981. 243p. $22.50. ISBN 0-939338-00-9. JC585 H847.

Describes nearly 400 organizations concerned with human rights in Latin America and the Caribbean, Asia, Africa, and the Middle East. Also includes a lengthy, annotated list of inter- and nongovernmental organizations located in North America and Europe concerned with these areas. A new edition will be published in early 1989.

Wiseberg, Laurie S., and Hazel Sirett, eds. **Human Rights Directory: Western Europe.** Washington, DC: Human Rights Internet, 1982. 334p. $30. ISBN 0-939338-01-7. JC599 E9H85.

Describes over 800 organizations in 25 countries of Western Europe working on human rights and social justice issues. As with other Human Rights Internet (HRI) directories, this one includes very detailed indexes.

Wiseberg, Laurie S., and Hazel Sirett, eds. **North American Human Rights Directory.** 3rd ed. Washington, DC: Human Rights Internet, 1984. 264p. $30. ISBN 0-939338-02-5. JC571 H76944.

This third edition of the North American Human Rights Internet (HRI) directory describes more than 700 U.S. and Canadian organizations concerned with human rights and social justice. The main section lists U.S. and Canadian organizations intermingled alphabetically by title, but there are several indexes that make it possible to access the information by different methods, e.g., acronym, geographic area, subject, etc.

World Directory of Human Rights Teaching and Research Institutions. Prepared at UNESCO by the Social and Human Science Documentation Centre and the Division of Human Rights and Peace. Paris: Unesco, 1988. Distributed by Berg Publishers, New York. 216p. $49.95. ISBN 0-85496-229-8. JC571 W89.

Presents basic information on institutions around the world, governmental and nongovernmental, that promote human rights research and teaching. Programs are identified and documented as to their nature, admission requirements, and scholarships offered. Information was obtained through a questionnaire developed by the Canadian Human Rights Foundation and sent to 10,000 institutions. Arranged by geographic region and then by country, subject of research or teaching, and scholarship aid.

Indexes and Abstracts

Alternative Press Index. Baltimore, MD: Alternative Press Center, 1969– .

Indexes over 200 alternative and radical publications, most not indexed elsewhere. Arranged by subject and then alphabetically by title. Uses the term *human rights,* which makes it easier to search than indexes that use only *civil rights.*

Historical Abstracts. Santa Barbara, CA: ABC-CLIO, 1955– .

Part B: Historical Abstracts, Twentieth Century Abstracts 1914 to the Present is very useful for human rights issues from a worldwide perspective. Approximately 20,000 articles are indexed in each volume, and beginning in 1980 selected new books and dissertations are listed. Arranged by general topic, by more specific topics, and by area or country with a special subject profile indexing system. Also available online.

Index to Legal Periodicals. Bronx, NY: H. W. Wilson, 1908– .

Published for the American Association of Law Librarians, this index covers most English language law publications, many of which have material on human rights. Cumulated volumes contain subject and author indexes. Also available online.

Legal Resource Index (LRI). Foster City, CA: Information Access Company, 1980– .

Co-sponsored by the American Association of Law Libraries, LRI provides subject, author, case name, and statute name access to over 700 major law journals in addition to seven legal newspapers. Helpful for many human rights issues. Also available online.

Public Affairs Information Service (PAIS) Bulletin. New York: PAIS, 1915– .

One of the best general indexes, the *PAIS Bulletin* is worldwide in scope and surveys approximately 1,400 journals and many other types of publications. It uses the term *human rights,* making searching considerably faster than when the material is grouped with that on *civil rights.* The online version is combined with the *Foreign Language Index* into *PAIS International.*

Religion Index One: Periodicals (RIO). Chicago, IL: ATLA Religion Indexes, 1949– .

Sponsored by the American Theological Library Association (ATLA), this index covers many human rights–related subjects. Over 380 journals are indexed, though a fair percentage are not in English. Its human rights topics are subdivided by country, which is often helpful for gaining a different perspective on human rights abuses in a specific country. Also available online.

Social Science Index. Bronx, NY: H. W. Wilson, 1974– .

Similar to the other Wilson indexes, this one covers the more traditional journals in the social sciences. There are author and subject entries and a separate section for book reviews. Also available online.

Sources of Human Rights Documents

Blaustein, Albert P., Roger Clark, and Jay A. Sigler, eds. **Human Rights Sourcebook.** New York: Paragon Institute Books, 1988. 970p. ISBN 0-88702-202-2. K3238 H86.

Designed for scholars, lawyers, teachers, and students, this volume contains the official texts of all the fundamental human rights documents. Additionally, there are explanations and commentaries and a three-page bibliography relating to the documents. Included are not only the U.N. instruments and Regional Covenants but sections of country constitutions relating to human and civil rights, copies of some important legislative items, judicial decisions, and miscellaneous documents, such as Czechoslovakia's *Charter 77.*

Brownlie, Ian, ed. **Basic Documents on Human Rights,** 2d ed. New York: Oxford University Press, 1981. 505p. $29.95 (paper). ISBN 0-198-876125-2. K3238 A1 B76.

This is one of the most useful volumes for basic documents, including those of the United Nations, the European Convention on Human Rights, and other regional documents. Includes introductory notes and biographical references. Index is valuable in tracing specific rights in many documents.

Buergenthal, Thomas, and Robert Norris. **Human Rights: The Inter-American System.** Dobbs Ferry, NY: Oceana Publications, 1982– . Looseleaf service. 4 binders. $85/binder. ISBN 0-379-20723-0. KDZ574 H85.

This title presents collected documents of conventions and conferences concerned with human rights in the inter-American system. The authors provide many treaties, statutes, and agreements covering the period 1901–1981, with commentaries. Each chapter has an introduction, with a selected bibliography at the end. Some basic documents, such as the Charter of the Organization of American States (OAS) and the American Declaration of the Rights and Duties of Man, are included.

Human Rights in International Law: Basic Texts. Strasbourg: Council of Europe, Directorate of Human Rights, 1985. 261p. Distributed by Manhattan Publishing Co., Croton, NY. ISBN 92-871-0399-2. K3238 H856.

Contains texts of the Universal Declaration of Human Rights, the International Covenants, and other U.N. documents. Texts of the Documents were prepared within the Council of Europe. Includes also the American Convention on Human Rights (1969), the African Charter of Human and People's Rights (1981), and the Final Act (Helsinki, 1975).

International Human Rights Instruments of the United Nations, 1948–1982. Collected and arranged by UNIFO Editorial Staff. London: Mansell Publishing, 1984. ISBN 0-7201-1698-8. K3238 I57.

Official texts of all major human rights international instruments adopted by the U.N. as of 1983, arranged in chronological order of adoption. A detailed subject index refers the user to specific documents, e.g., "asylum from persecution" is treated in five different documents. Includes tables showing signatories, ratifications, accessions, and declarations by country for each document.

Joyce, James Avery, ed. **Human Rights: International Documents.** Dobbs Ferry, NY: Oceana Publications, 1978. 3 vols. $50/vol. ISBN 0-379-20395-2. JC571 J65.

Beginning with the U.N. documents in Volume I, the editor presents a compilation of human rights instruments issued in the 30 years since the Universal Declaration of Human Rights. Volume II is on selected topics and specific countries. The works of intergovernmental and nongovernmental agencies and organizations are found in Volume III. One of the most comprehensive collections of human rights instruments for the time period covered.

United Nations Centre for Human Rights. **Human Rights: A Compilation of International Instruments.** New York: United Nations, 1988. 414p. $30. ISBN 92-1-154066-6.

An updated version of earlier compilations of human rights instruments published by the United Nations Centre for Human Rights in Geneva. This edition includes instruments adopted up to December 31, 1987. In addition to U.N. instruments, there are some by two of its agencies—the International Labour Organisation (ILO) and the United Nations Educational, Scientific, and Cultural Organization (UNESCO). A list of instruments in chronological order of adoption is appended.

U.S. Committee on Foreign Affairs. **Human Rights Documents.** Washington, DC: Government Printing Office, 1983. 774p. J3238 H853.

A compilation of basic human rights laws and international instruments pertaining to human rights. Included are the Declaration of Independence, the U.S. Constitution, and excerpts from current U.S. statutes relating to human rights. Part II contains U.N. human rights instruments and some regional instruments, such as the European Convention on Human Rights.

Thesaurus

Stormorken, Bjorn, and Leo Zwaak. **Human Rights Terminology in International Law: A Thesaurus.** Dordrecht, The Netherlands: Martinus Nijhoff, 1987. Distributed by Kluwer Academic Publishers, Norwell, MA. 234p. $52. ISBN 90-247-3643-9. K3239.3 S76.

A thesaurus of human rights terms as found in the most important human rights documents, such as the Universal Declaration of Human Rights, the European Convention on Human Rights, and the African Charter of Human and People's Rights. Four lists are given: the master alphabetical list, in which terms are followed by hierarchical information on interrelationships with other terms; a simple alphabetical list for quick reference; a KWOC (Keyword Out of Context) list; and a list by number of articles in each of the human rights documents cited.

Yearbooks and Encyclopedia

Israel Yearbook on Human Rights. Tel Aviv, Israel: Tel Aviv University Faculty of Law. Annual. $12. ISSN 0333-5925.

Published under the auspices of the Faculty of Law at the Tel Aviv University, this yearbook contains articles by different scholars describing aspects of human rights in Europe, America, and Israel. Included also are judgments relating to the Administrative Territories in specific cases.

Osmanczyk, Edmund Jan. **The Encyclopedia of the United Nations and International Agreements.** Philadelphia: Taylor and Francis, 1985. 1059p. $160. ISBN 0-85066-312-1. JX1977 O8213.

This work brings together in encyclopedia arrangement a compendium of political, economic, and social information related to the U.N. It contains many references to and some texts of human rights documents and covenants. Useful for identifying various instruments and commissions related to them.

United Nations. **Yearbook on Human Rights.** New York: United Nations. Issued annually 1946–1972; biennially 1974–1978. ISBN 92-1-154051-8. JC571 U4.

Last issue published for 1979 in 1986. Arranged in three parts: (1) material reflecting legislative, administrative, judicial, and other national measures and court decisions taken from government reports submitted under the U.N. instruments; (2) reports of supervisory bodies and agencies established under the international instruments; and (3) brief accounts of human rights developments and activities in the U.N. system.

Monographs

The following is a selective list of monographs in the field of human rights published since 1983 by governmental and nongovernmental agencies and by research scholars, academicians, and activists.

Alderson, J. **Human Rights and the Police.** Strasbourg: Council of Europe, 1984. 214p. ISBN 92-871-0365-8. K3240.4 A44.

This title is designed to introduce the concept of human rights to those involved in police work and to show its relevance to police activity. Basing his discussion on those rights defined in the European Convention on Human Rights and the case law of its supervisory organs, the author demonstrates methods of integrating human rights issues into police training on all levels.

Alexeyeva, Ludmilla. **Soviet Dissent: Contemporary Movements for National, Religious and Human Rights.** Middletown, CT: Wesleyan University Press, 1985. 521p. $35. ISBN 0-8195-5124. $15.95 (paper). ISBN 0-8195-6176-2. HV527 A4713.

Based on her years in the Soviet Union as a Communist editor for government publishing houses and later as a human rights activist in the United States, the author describes the independent movements of dissent in the Soviet Union, e.g., the movements for emigration, religious liberty, and social and economic justice. Her research is based on the *samizdat* (underground publishing) in the *Chronicle of Human Events*, documents of public associations and interviews with many of those in the dissident movement.

Americas Watch

See page 37 for a description of this organization. The following are book-length publications of Americas Watch. These are arranged by country, except for one title of general interest. Briefer reports are listed under the description of Americas Watch in Chapter 4.

General

With Friends Like These: The Americas Watch Report on Human Rights and U.S. Policy in Latin America. New York: Pantheon Books, 1985. 281p. $8.95. ISBN 0-394-72949-8. JC599 L3 W58.

Documents the human rights situation in nine Latin American countries—Argentina, Chile, Uruguay, El Salvador, Nicaragua, Honduras, Guatemala, Colombia, and Peru—and demonstrates how the present U.S. administration has blatantly abused, ignored, or misrepresented concern for human rights by pursuing political and military goals in these countries.

Chile

Chile: Human Rights and the Plebiscite. July 1988. 255p. $15. ISBN 0-938579-64-9.

This report focuses on the laws and procedures which govern the presidential plebiscite in Chile and the constitutional framework which defines a future "democracy" for Chile in the context of human rights conditions. It notes the extraordinary degree of intimidation that prevails at the time of the elections. Under the 1980 Constitution, political rights would continue to be restricted in the future and the military will have a permanent role in the government.

Chile since the Coup: Ten Years of Repression. August 25, 1983. 137p. $7. ISBN 0-938579-002-2.

Based on research by Americas Watch representatives in Chile, extensive U.N. documentation, and data from Chilean human rights organizations, the report deals with the characteristics and trends of human rights violations in Chile since 1973, with particular emphasis on the institutional nature of repression, from legal manipulations to the pervasiveness of surveillance and torture.

Colombia

The Central-Americanization of Colombia? January 1986. 146p. $8. ISBN 0-938579-01-0.

This report examines the peace process initiated by President Belisario Betancur, the forces that undermined it, and its relationship to human rights violations in Colombia during the three previous years. The report points out that Columbia needs civilian control of the military, meaningful punishment for human rights violators, economic reform, and an authentic political role for dissident groups.

El Salvador

The Civilian Toll, 1986–1987. Ninth Supplement to the Report on Human Rights in El Salvador, August 30, 1987. 325p. $15. ISBN 9-938579-35-5.

Focusing on some of the notable episodes of human rights violations during the first several months of 1987, this report discusses the roles played by the military and the guerrillas, treatment of civilians, displaced repatriates and relocatees, security forces, death squads, and the effect of U.S. policy in El Salvador.

The Continuing Terror. September 1985. 156p. $10. ISBN 0-938579-02-9.

Following other Americas Watch reports on El Salvador, this one describes the human rights situation during the first half of 1985. The practices of the government continue to include violations of the laws of war and other abuses of human rights that are not directly connected to combat. These include aerial bombardments that hit civilians, forced relocations, harassment of health facilities, a resurgence of the death squads, and the continuing use of torture by security forces.

Free Fire: A Report on Human Rights in El Salvador. August 1984. 148p. $6. (With the Lawyers Committee for Human Rights.)

Although there was a marked decline in killings and disappearances after Duarte became president, indiscriminate attacks by the Salvadoran armed forces on civilian noncombatants in conflict zones continued. Evidence cited in this report shows that these attacks are part of a deliberate policy to force civilians from these zones and thereby deprive guerrillas of civilian support. Includes responses of the U.S. State Department to questions regarding these attacks.

Labor Rights in El Salvador. March 1988. 117p. $8. ISBN 0-938579-60-6.

This is the first comprehensive report on violations of labor rights in El Salvador. It describes systemic repression of trade unions and peasant organizations, which includes in the year 1987 alone nine assassinations, five disappearances, the military occupation of farms and worksites, dozens of arrests of union and farm workers, limits to the right to collective bargaining and the right to strike and the use of military force to suppress legitimate union activity.

Land Mines in El Salvador and Nicaragua: The Civilian Victims. December 1986. 117p. $8. ISBN 0-938579-29-0.

The use of land mines by both conventional and guerrilla forces has had a devastating effect on the civilian population in El Salvador and Nicaragua. This report describes the casualties in both countries and presents a comprehensive analysis of the international law governing the use of these weapons. Makes recommendations for avoiding further civilian casualties.

Settling into Routine: Human Rights in Duarte's Second Year. May 1986. 162p. $10. ISBN 0-938579-19-3.

Because the gross violations of human rights in the early 1980s had abated somewhat and there were fewer deaths, the acceptance of some abuses had become routine. The facts reported here show that torture, forced confessions, pillaging, and executions are still very prevalent. The treatment of human rights abuses by both the Salvadoran government and the U.S. Embassy is covered.

Guatemala

Civil Patrols in Guatemala. August 1986. 105p. $6. ISBN 0-938579-20-7.

This publication traces the development of the Civil Patrols—the role they play, who belongs, and the economic, cultural, and psychological effects they have on the people of Guatemala. Includes a copy of the Civil Patrol Code of Conduct.

Guatemala: A Nation of Prisoners. January 1984. 260p. $10.

This report focuses on the developments that have taken place during the first five months of General Oscar Mejía Victores' rule, but it also shows the cumulative consequences of military rule in Guatemala. Includes the role of the courts, the church, and the United States.

Guatemalan Refugees in Mexico, 1980–1984. September 1984. 104p. $10. ISBN 0-938579-08-8.

The report describes the plight of refugees driven from Guatemala because of the terrible human rights abuses there and criticizes Mexico's treatment of the refugees, particularly its policy of forcible repatriation, which became necessary because of the Guatemalan military's cross-border raids. Points out that Mexico is now making efforts to improve its protection of refugees.

Human Rights in Guatemala during President Cerezo's First Year. February 1987. 108p. $8. ISBN 0-938579-31-2. (With the British Parliamentary Human Rights Group.)

Despite Guatemala's having the worst record for sustained and pervasive political violence of any country in the hemisphere, there were hopes for an era of commitment to human dignity when President Cerezo came to power. Although the president is personally committed to human rights, this report asserts that he is not willing to expose the abuses of the past and punish those responsible for violations.

Honduras

Human Rights in Honduras: Central America's Sideshow. May 1987. 150p. $8. ISBN 0-938579-33-9.

Despite six years of civilian rule, Honduras remains a country where the security forces routinely torture detainees and where several people are killed for apparently political reasons each year. The report includes material on the Honduran government's treatment of refugees and the CIA's role in disappearances in the early 1980s.

Nicaragua

Human Rights in Nicaragua: August 1987 to August 1988. August 1988. 128p. $10. ISBN 0-929692-01-2.

Violations of the laws of war by both sides declined in number since the signing of the ceasefire in March 1988, but some violations continue. This Americas Watch report cites the termination of the state of emergency as the most important improvement brought about by the peace process. It calls on both the Nicaraguan government and the Contras to vigorously prosecute any personnel for gross abuses of human rights.

Human Rights in Nicaragua during 1986. February 1987. 120p. $8. ISBN 0-938579-30-4.

This report assesses the status of civil and political rights as well as the violations of the laws of war by both sides in Nicaragua's armed conflict from February to December 1986. Violations by the Contras—including indiscriminate attacks against civilians, systematic killings of persons believed to represent the government, and widespread kidnapping—continued to cause great suffering to the Nicaraguan people. The government persists in violating internationally accepted standards of human rights, such as the right to due process, but does not engage in systematic violations of the laws of war in the course of military operations.

Paraguay

Rule by Fear: Paraguay after Thirty Years under Stroessner. January 1985. 104p. $8. ISBN 0-938579-15-0.

Based on an Americas Watch mission sent to Paraguay at the request of that nation's government, this report details human rights abuses relating to freedom of the press, the administration of justice, and union and land disputes in a country controlled by the world's then senior military dictator, General Alfredo Stroessner.

Peru

Abdicating Democratic Authority: Human Rights in Peru. October 1984. 162p. $8. ISBN 0-938579-17-7.

The report describes the intolerable situation that exists in Peru—a country facing gross human right abuses from both the government and the Sendero Luminoso (Shining Path), one of the most brutal guerrilla organizations in the world. The strong leadership needed to stop the government from fighting terrorism with counterterrorism has not been provided. The report notes that both those within and outside the country have for the most part remained silent about the necessity for real progress in counteracting human rights violations.

Human Rights in Peru after President Garcia's First Year. September 1986. 119p. $8. ISBN 0-938579-25-8.

President Garcia's inaugural message made references to a new policy that proposed to instill a scrupulous respect for human rights within the conduct of the government's counterinsurgency campaign. According to this report, the country experienced a dramatic change regarding human rights over the first year: there was a noticeable decrease in cases of disappearances, extrajudicial executions, and indiscriminate killings attributable to the security forces in the emergency zone. Abuses do still occur, however, and there are few successful attempts to punish violators.

Amnesty International

See page 38 for a description of this organization. The following are book-length publications of Amnesty International. Briefer reports are listed under the description of Amnesty International in Chapter 4.

Argentina: The Military Juntas and Human Rights. 1987. 100p. $5. ISBN 0-939994-34-8.

This is a detailed account of the remarkable trial of former Junta members—nine military commanders who ruled Argentina before a civilian government was elected in 1983, during what was termed the "dirty war" against subversion.

Disappearances. 1981. 168p. $4.95. ISBN 0-939994-00-3. HV6762 A3 D57.

Provides case studies of "disappearances" that have occurred in Argentina, Guatemala, some of the African countries, Afghanistan, and the Philippines and analyzes the structures and agencies responsible for them.

Political Killings by Governments. London, 1983. 131p. $5. ISBN 0-86210-051-8. JC571 P59.

This work reports on the unlawful and brutal killing by government authorities of hundreds of thousands of persons in many countries. It gives detailed accounts of such atrocities in Guatemala, Indonesia, Kampuchea, Uganda, Argentina, India, and Libya. Includes a discussion of international legal standards and makes recommendations for non-governmental bodies interested in preventing these flagrant violations.

South Korea: Violations of Human Rights. 1986. 109p. $5. ISBN 0-939994-21-6.

This report presents detailed case histories highlighting the plight of individual victims of human rights abuses. Thousands of persons have been detained in Korea—of those who confessed to crimes they did not commit, some were executed and others served long prison terms. Amnesty urges the government to protect the rights of its citizens against such violations.

Torture in the Eighties. 1984. 263p. $5.95 ISBN 0-939994-06-2.

This is a major Amnesty report that presents detailed evidence of systematic torture during interrogation and covers a wide range of abuses, including electric shock, severe beatings, and mock executions. Analyzing the conditions under which torture takes place, the report spells out a global program for its abolition.

Voices for Freedom. 1986. 208p. $15. ISBN 0-939994-20-8.

Spanning two and one-half decades of contemporary history and sketching a remarkable portrait of human rights in dozens of countries, this book records the work of Amnesty International and portrays the lives of the people it has sought to protect. Illustrated with numerous documentary photographs.

Asia Watch

See page 39 for a description of this organization. The following are book-length publications of Asia Watch. Briefer reports are listed under the description of Asia Watch in Chapter 4.

Cycles of Violence: Human Rights in Sri Lanka since the Indo–Sri Lanka Agreement. 1987. 131p. $10. ISBN 0-938579-43-6.

This report describes the situation in Sri Lanka, particularly from 1983 to 1987, when India and Sri Lanka signed an accord. Several years of intense fighting between armed Tamil militants and the predominantly Sinhalese Sri Lankan security forces resulted in many violations of international human rights by both sides. Asia Watch makes several recommendations to bring the violations to an end—among them that the Sri Lankan government permit the Red Cross access to the country.

Human Rights in Taiwan, 1986–1987. December 1987. 269p. $12. ISBN 0-938579-70-3.

Significant progress has been made in the human rights situation in Taiwan, a country ruled by an authoritarian government for 38 years. Many political prisoners have been released, an opposition party has been formed, and the government has lifted martial law. The Taiwanese people are still deprived of many of their civil and political rights, however. This Asia Watch report calls for an end to such repressions as the mistreatment of criminals and suspects, political interference in the judiciary, and restrictions on the freedom of expression.

A Stern Steady Crackdown: Legal Process and Human Rights in South Korea. May 1987. 133p. $8.

This report reviews some of the major events of 1986 in South Korea as a background for understanding the rationale behind government abuses of internationally accepted human rights. These violations include arrests without warrants or reasonable grounds to believe a crime has been committed, denial of prisoner access to lawyers and family, refusal to reveal the location of detainees, and the continued use of torture. Asia Watch calls on the government to end these abuses and to return documents collected by an American in the course of preparing this report that were confiscated by South Korean officials at the time she left the country.

Best Friends; Violations of Human Rights in Liberia, America's Closest Ally in Africa. New York: Fund for Free Expression, May 1986. 64p. $5. ISBN 0-938579-46-0.

This report on human rights conditions in Liberia is based on two visits made to that country by Michael Massing in 1985 and 1986. Interviews conducted with government officials, opposition leaders, journalists, church officials, business leaders, and U.S. diplomats confirmed massive and continuing violations of human rights. Notes that the U.S. policy of quiet diplomacy has done little to improve the conditions in that country.

Bloed, A., and P. Van Dijk. **Essays on Human Rights in the Helsinki Process.** The Hague: Martinus Nijhoff, 1985. 145p. ISBN 90-247-3211-5. K3240.6 E85.

Dutch legal scholars discuss human rights issues and humanitarian problems against the background of the Madrid Conference of 1983 and its document. Includes essays on trade union freedom, jamming of foreign radio broadcasts, and the 1980 Moscow Olympic Games boycott.

Buergenthal, Thomas. **Protecting Human Rights in the Americas: Selected Problems,** 2d ed. Strasbourg: Kehl, 1986. Distributed by Engel Publishers, Arlington, VA. 389p. ISBN 3-88357-055-9. JC585 B83.

Presents historical evolution of the inter-American system for the protection of human rights (which derived from the Charter of the Organization of American States) and the entry into force of the American Convention on Human Rights of 1978. The book includes chapters on how rights are protected and what implementing mechanisms are used. Specific problems such as the suspension of guarantees and the impact and effectiveness of the system are discussed. Appendix contains basic documents relating to the Americas.

Campbell, Tom, ed. **Human Rights: From Rhetoric to Reality.** New York: Basil Blackwell, 1986. 262p. $45. ISBN 0-631-14361-0. K3240.4 H836.

Contributors explore the ways in which the rhetoric of the ideas expressed in the Universal Declaration of Human Rights can be applied to the reality of specific social circumstances in a manner that can be both accurately monitored and adjudicated in a court of law. Women's rights, labor union rights, the rights of the mentally ill, and the right to public assembly are some of the cases covered.

Campbell, Tom. **The Left and Rights: A Conceptual Analysis of the Idea of Socialist Rights.** Boston: Routledge and Kegan Paul, 1983. 253p. $10. ISBN 0-7100-9085-4. K3240.4 C36.

This book undertakes an investigation of whether there is a philosophically acceptable theory of rights that would be applicable to both socialist and nonsocialist systems of thought. If there is, the author believes the formation of a set of common concepts would help to resolve ideological conflicts concerning social and economic policy.

Catholic Institute for International Relations. **Nicaragua: The Right to Survive.** London: The Catholic Institute for International Relations, 1987. Distributed by North River Press, Croton-on-Hudson, NY. 135p. $9.95. ISBN 0-88422-074-2. JC599 N5 N555.

An attempt to present an overview of the human rights situation in Nicaragua, this work builds on the issues raised by other human rights groups, such as Americas Watch and Amnesty International. It examines the Contra war and the Sandinista response, the state of emergency, restrictions on civil liberties, and press censorship. Also covered are the judicial and penal systems, the relationship between the government and the churches, and Sandinista activity relating to the Miskito Indians.

Cohen, Esther Rosalind. **Human Rights in the Israeli-Occupied Territories, 1967–1982** (Melland Schill Monographs in International Law). Dover, NH: Manchester University Press, 1985. 290p. $45. ISBN 0-7190-1726-2. JC599 I68.

Originally written as a Ph.D. thesis, this work examines the application and interaction of two bodies of international rules—those forming part of the law of armed conflict governing belligerent occupation and those developed by the modern trend to give legal recognition and protection to basic human rights. Covers such issues as the Israeli settlement on the West Bank, dismissal of local mayors, security measures, freedom of religion, and social and economic policies.

Cohn, Haim Hermann. **Human Rights in Jewish Law.** New York: KTAV Publishing House, 1984. 266p. $25. ISBN 0-88125-036-8. BN95 C661h.

Published for the Institute of Jewish Affairs in London, this work presents Jewish legal history as it relates to 25 specific human rights noted in the Universal Declaration of Human Rights. Concludes that the duties imposed by Jewish lawgivers reflect their ethical standards in much the same way the rights enumerated in the Universal Declaration reflect the ethical standards of the founders of the U.N.

Copper, John F., Michael Franzo, and Yuan-li Wu. **Human Rights in Post-Mao China** (Westview Studies in China and East Asia). Boulder, CO: Westview Press, 1985. 117p. $20.50. ISBN 0-8133-0182-3. JQ1516 C66.

Investigates human rights in China from a historical perspective, but concentrates on the period since the death of Mao in 1976. The authors analyze legal practices and institutions, intellectual and ideological policies, and economic changes implemented under Deng's leadership in order to evaluate the degree to which there have been real changes in the Chinese attitude toward human rights. They also examine conflicts between policies of modernization and limitations on individual freedoms typical in Communist societies. Appendix contains an analysis of over 2,300 arrests.

Desmond, Cosmas. **Persecution East and West: Human Rights, Political Prisoners and Amnesty.** New York: Penguin Books, 1983, 172p. ISBN 0-140-52345-6. JC571 D48.

This is a personal reflection on some of the questions raised by the author's experiences as director of the British Section of Amnesty International. He was personally involved in the struggle against apartheid. Analyzes both the capitalist and socialist oppression of human rights and the efforts of Amnesty International and the U.N. to defend human rights.

Donnelly, Jack. **The Concept of Human Rights.** New York: St. Martin's Press, 1985. 120p. $25.50. ISBN 0-312-15941-2. JC571 D74.

Based on the author's Ph.D. dissertation, this work discusses the nature and source of human rights, competing theories and approaches, the limitations of the state in an individual's human rights, and particular questions regarding Third World concepts of human rights.

Donnelly, Jack, and Rhoda E. Howard, eds. **International Handbook of Human Rights.** Westport, CT: Greenwood Press, 1987. 505p. $56. ISBN 0-313-24788-9. JC571 I587.

The editors present case studies of national human rights practices in several countries that represent a variety of political systems. Most chapters are by political scientists and sociologists knowledgeable about human rights in the countries they describe. Notes that many human rights violations are perpetrated by states against their own citizens.

Drinan, Robert F. **Cry of the Oppressed: The History and Hope of the Human Rights Revolution.** New York: Harper and Row, 1987. 210p. $17.95. ISBN 0-06-250261-1. K3240.4 D74.

As a law professor at Georgetown University and former member of Congress, the author taught a course on international human rights for several years. In this book, which is based on the course, he describes the legal, moral, spiritual, and religious roots of human rights. Covers the human rights movement as it has grown since World War II, the role of the many human rights organizations, and the possibility of a permanent international court.

Drzemczewski, Andrew Z. **European Human Rights Convention in Domestic Law: A Comparative Study.** New York: Oxford University Press, 1983. 372p. $63. ISBN 0-19-825396-6. $19.95 (paper). ISBN 0-19-825525-X. K3236 D79.

This book presents an analysis of the way in which the member states of the Council of Europe provide for incorporation into their own law of their obligations under the European Convention on Human Rights.

Edwards, R. Randle, Louis Henkin, and Andrew J. Nathan. **Human Rights in Contemporary China.** A Study of the East Asian Institute and of the Center for the Study of Human Rights, Columbia University. New York: Columbia University Press, 1986. 208p. $27.50. ISBN 0-231-06180-3. JC599 C6 E39.

The three authors present separate analyses of human rights in contemporary China, seen in international and comparative perspective. Henkin compares Chinese commitment to human rights to ideas of the United States and the United Nations; Edwards analyzes Chinese theory and practice as they apply to human rights; and Nathan focuses on basic political rights.

Evans, Robert, and Alice Evans. **Human Rights: A Dialogue between First and Third Worlds.** Maryknoll, NY: Orbis, 1983. 264p. $9.95. ISBN 0-88344-194-2. BT738.15 H85.

In order to contribute to bridging the gap between the First and Third Worlds, the authors developed a project of research and education to help in the understanding of human rights problems from a global perspective. They present eight case studies representing different areas of the world, each focusing on a specific human rights issue. Priority is given in the selection of cases to those involving the basic rights of survival and liberation.

Forsythe, David. **Human Rights and World Politics.** Lincoln, NE: University of Nebraska Press, 1983. 309p. $25.95. ISBN 0-8032-1962-8. JC571 F634.

Writing for students and the interested general reader, the author describes and evaluates the major values found in human rights treaties; analyzes U.S. policy relating to human rights and the role of private groups working for human rights during the 1970s and early 1980s; also discusses the political philosophies underlying the global debate about human rights. Argues that action on behalf of human rights is possible despite differences in political philosophy.

Fowler, Michael. **Thinking about Human Rights: Contending Approaches to Human Rights in U.S. Foreign Policy.** Lanham, MD: University Press of America, 1987. $24.75. ISBN 0-8191-5818-6. $12.50 (paper). ISBN 0-8191-5819-4. E840 F68.

The author compares and contrasts the views of prominent individuals on the fundamental issues raised by American human rights policies. The individuals are grouped into four categories: Traditional Thinkers, Revisionist Thinkers, Legal-Order Thinkers, and Bipolar Thinkers. The drawbacks and benefits of each to human rights are shown.

Frundt, Henry J. **Refreshing Pauses: Coca-Cola and Human Rights in Guatemala.** New York: Praeger Publishers, 1987. 288p. $34.85. ISBN 0-275-92764-4. JC599 G8 F78.

This book describes the struggle by workers at the Guatemala Coca-Cola bottling plant from 1976 to 1986 and examines the reasons the union was able to survive and become instrumental in strengthening the union movement in the country. Roles of the Catholic Church and international investment companies are also examined.

Gastil, Raymond D., ed. **Freedom in the World: Political Rights and Civil Liberties, 1985–86** (Freedom House Annual Series). Westport, CT: Greenwood Press, 1987. 438p. $35. ISBN 0-313-25398-6. JC571 G336.

Published irregularly since 1979, this work attempts to evaluate human rights ratings of individual countries in the Comparative Survey of Freedom, which focuses on various aspects of human freedom. Includes essays on current issues and Country Summaries, which give brief statements on the political rights and civil liberties of particular countries and make comparisons among them.

Gewirth, Alan. **Human Rights: Essays on Justifications and Applications.** Chicago: University of Chicago Press, 1983. 366p. $35. ISBN 0-226-28877-3. JC571 G44.

This is a collection of fourteen essays published by the author between 1970 and 1982. The first six deal primarily with the problems of justifying the moral principle that all human beings have equal rights. The remaining eight discuss applications of the principle to some important issues of human life, society, and government. The collected essays represent the author's contribution, from a philosophical point of view, to the development of a comprehensive theory of human rights.

Gruenwald, Oskar, and Karen Rosenblum-Cole, eds. **Human Rights in Yugoslavia.** New York: Irvington Publications, 1986. 673p. ISBN 0-8290-1770-4. JC599 Y8 H36.

The first comprehensive, multidisciplinary volume describing dissent and human rights in Yugoslavia, this work grew out of a panel on the subject held during the American Political Science Association Conference in 1979. Some of the issues covered are political prisons in Yugoslavia's Gulag Archipelago, the secret police, self-determination, human rights of women, and the role of dissent in Yugoslavia. The final section contains documentary material, such as copies of petitions to government officials regarding grievances, with the names of the signers.

Hannum, Hurst, ed. **Guide to International Human Rights Practice.** Published for the International Human Rights Law Group. Philadelphia: University of Pennsylvania Press, 1984. 310p. $14.95 (paper). ISBN 0-812-21150-2. K3240.4 G94.

The International Human Rights Law Group, composed of distinguished lawyers and scholars who have consultative status with the U.N. Economic and Social Council, had this volume prepared to assist lawyers, NGOs (nongovernmental organizations), and individuals in using the growing number of procedures available to redress violations of human rights.

Hannum, Hurst. **The Right To Leave and Return in International Law and Practice** (International Studies in Human Rights, no. 8). The Hague: Martinus Nijhoff, 1987. Distributed by Kluwer Academic Publishers, Hingham, MA. 189p. $62.50. ISBN 90-247-3445-2. K3265 H36.

Written by a scholar in the field of human rights, this work is a thorough analysis and systematic critique of the right of freedom of movement—a right once considered secondary rather than fundamental. The author suggests a number of steps that interested bodies, national governments, and nongovernmental groups can take to guarantee the effective realization of this basic human right. The work contains texts of various documents relating to this right.

Helsinki Watch

See page 44 for a description of this organization. The following are book-length publications of Helsinki Watch. Briefer reports are listed under the description of Helsinki Watch in Chapter 4.

From Below: Independent Peace and Environmental Movements in Eastern Europe and the USSR. October 1987. 263p. $12. ISBN 0-938579-67-3.

This work describes some of the events that led to a more "civil society" (a term denoting a society in which independent discussion and criticism can take place and in which an effort can be made to restrict the state's use of power) in Eastern Europe. Some of these events were the signing of the Helsinki accords, the growth of Solidarity in Poland, the rise of a vigorous Western peace movement, and the nuclear disaster in Chernobyl—all of which had some effect on the human rights situation in Eastern European countries.

State of Flux: Human Rights in Turkey. December 1987. 143p. $8. ISBN 0-938579-68-1.

This, the sixth report on human rights in Turkey issued by Helsinki Watch, concludes that, while positive steps have been taken in some areas of human rights, they are undermined by negative actions such as the continued use of torture in police detention and the incarceration of many thousands of political prisoners. These actions stem partially from the repressive 1982 Constitution and from equally repressive laws. Also discusses of human rights abuses of Kurdish minorities.

Holleman, Warren Lee. **The Human Rights Movement: Western Values and Theological Perspectives.** New York: Praeger Publishers, 1987. 256p. $37.85. ISBN 0-275-92789-X. JC585 H755.

The author examines the reasons human rights abuses continue to increase and suggests that part of the problem is the fact that Western and non-Western nations do not agree on the meaning of human rights and on the means of preserving them. The importance of theological ethics as a basis for dialogue is stressed.

Howard, Rhoda E. **Human Rights in Commonwealth Africa.** Totowa, NJ: Rowman and Littlefield, 1986. 264p. $34.50. ISBN 0-8476-7433-9. $12.95 (paper). ISBN 0-8476-7434-7. JC599 A36 H68.

This volume analyzes the social-structural factors that affect human rights in nine Commonwealth African countries: Gambia, Sierra Leone, Ghana, and Nigeria in West Africa; Kenya, Malawi, Tanzania, Uganda, and Zambia in East and Central Africa. These countries, though different, are sufficiently similar to make it possible to study them as a group. Included are discussions on economic, communal, political, and civil rights, with a separate chapter on women's rights.

Hsiung, James C., ed. **Human Rights in East Asia: A Cultural Perspective.** New York: Paragon House Publishers, 1985. 165p. $12.95. ISBN 0-88702-208-1. JC599 E18 H85.

This work attempts to answer the question of whether human rights have the same meaning in the cultural-political context of East Asia as in the West, using three models to offer a limited comparative view: the Western adversarial model, the Oriental consensual model, and the Oriental Communist model. Five countries are examined: Japan, Taiwan, South Korea, the People's Republic of China, and North Korea.

Hull, Elizabeth. **Without Justice for All: The Constitutional Rights of Aliens** (Contributions in Political Science no. 129). Westport, CT: Greenwood Press, 1985. 244p. $35. ISBN 0-313-23670-4. KF4800 H84.

The author examines the way American law and legal practice affect the country's noncitizens, including immigrants, nonimmigrants, and undocumented illegal aliens. She shows the inconsistency of U.S. policy, which gives asylum to 99 percent of those fleeing Communist governments but to only a token number from right-wing repressive governments. Points out that certain classes of people are excluded—sometimes on unjust grounds.

Human Rights in the Homelands: South Africa's Delegation of Repression. New York: Fund for Free Expression, 1984. 149p. $8. ISBN 0-938579-47-9.

South Africa, in establishing mini-states known as "homelands," has deprived the Blacks of their South African nationality. They are regarded in South African law as temporary sojourners in the land of their birth—a policy unknown in modern times except for the denationalization of the Jews by the Germans in 1941. This report examines not only this denial of rights but also the repressive practices of officials delegated to be the ostensible rulers of the homelands. Conditions were especially difficult for young rural blacks who had no local employment opportunities but were prevented from going into the cities to find work.

Human Rights Watch

See page 46 for a description of this organization. The following are book-length publications of Human Rights Watch. Briefer reports are listed under the description of Human Rights Watch in Chapter 4.

Critique: Review of the Department of State's Country Reports on Human Rights Practices for 1987. June 1988. 192p. $12. ISBN 0-938579-63-0. (With the Lawyers Committee for Human Rights.)

This is the ninth annual *Critique* of the U.S. State Department's *Country Reports* by Human Rights Watch. (Earlier publications are under Americas Watch with slightly different titles for different years.) It is noted that while some of the country reports are "models of even-handedness," many are written with U.S. policy considerations being given primary emphasis. Thus human rights reports of perceived allies are oftentimes softened in their emphasis while those of perceived adversaries are made worse than other human rights groups have found them. Reviews of country reports are arranged alphabetically by country.

The Persecution of Human Rights Monitors, December 1987 to December 1988: A Worldwide Survey. December 1988. 218p. $15. ISBN 0-929692-09-4.

This publication shows the extent to which citizens of repressive countries all over the world have taken up the effort to monitor their governments' human rights practices. Since the previous report in 1987, 30 human rights monitors were killed or died in custody, 3 were "disappeared," and 20 others who were not human rights monitors were killed because of their connections to human rights monitors. In all, the report lists 750 cases of human rights monitors who were persecuted by 62 governments or armed groups attempting to overthrow governments or crush some challenge to the government or their own privileged positions.

The Reagan Administration's Record on Human Rights in 1988. January 1989. 245p. $12. 0-929692-11-X. (With the Lawyers Committee for Human Rights.)

This work is the seventh and final report on the human rights record of the Reagan administration. It shows the considerable evolution in human rights policy during the eight years: from opposing most attempts to promote human rights to helping institutionalize the stated commitment to human rights as part of U.S. policy. It provides an overview of U.S. responses to human rights violations in 42 countries, arranged alphabetically by country. It also includes chapters on U.S. human rights laws and treaties, the United Nations, and refugee, asylum, and immigration policy.

Humana, Charles. **World Human Rights Guide.** New York: Facts on File, 1986. 344p. $35. ISBN 0-8160-1404-3. JC571 H788.

An updated edition of an earlier work assessing the human rights performances of 120 countries, this report is based on the results of a questionnaire that sought information on 40 items, including such freedoms as peaceful political opposition, political and legal equality for women, travel within and outside one's own country, independent publishing and newspapers, and the practice of one's religion. The report gives each country a percentage rating on its attainment of human rights according to concepts in U.N. covenants.

Humphrey, John P. **Human Rights and the U.N.: A Great Adventure.** Ardsley-on-Hudson, NY: Transnational Publishers, 1984. 350p. $40. ISBN 0-941320-14-6. K3240.4 H85.

The author, who served during 1946 to 1966 as the first director of the U.N.'s Division of Human Rights, gives a personal account of that body's role in the protection and promotion of human rights, including some of the facts regarding the drafting of the U.N. Declaration of Human Rights, the various covenants, and the Convention on Racial Discrimination. Shows some of the difficulties of working through human rights documents during the Cold War period.

Iwe, Nwachukwuike S. S. **The History and Content of Human Rights: A Study of History and Interpretation of Human Rights** (American University Studies, Series IX, Vol. 11). New York: Peter Lang Publishers, 1986. 414p. $46.30. ISBN 0-8204-0298-2. JC571 I86.

The author, a Nigerian professor, traces in great detail the development and interpretation of human rights from the time of the Greek and Roman Empires through the Middle Ages to the twentieth century. Documents the role played by Christianity, particularly the Catholic Church, and explores the roles of international and interterritorial agencies and organizations.

Jonas, Susanne, Ed McCaughan, and Elizabeth Sutherland Martinez, eds. **Guatemala, Tyranny on Trial: Testimony of the Permanent People's Tribunal.** San Francisco: Synthesis Publications, 1984. 336p. $19.95. ISBN 0-89935-032-1. $9.95 (paper). ISBN 0-89935-024-0. JC599 G8 P47.

This volume presents a translation of the proceedings of the three-day session of the Permanent People's Tribunal on Guatemala held in

Madrid in 1983. The presenters, who gave overviews of the many types of human rights violations in Guatemala, were followed by individuals who gave eyewitness testimony that corroborated and exemplified statements of the presenters. The Tribunal concluded that there was a systematic violation of fundamental human rights by the Guatemalan military dictatorship. The editors hoped to expose the harsh truth about these violations by the U.S.-supported Guatemalan government.

Kanger, Helle. **Human Rights in the U.N. Declaration.** Uppsala: Acta Universitatis Upsaliensis, 1984. Distributed by Almquist and Wiksell International in Sweden. 208p. ISBN 91-554-1548-2. K3240.4 K27.

An analysis of the rights enumerated in the U.N. Declaration of Human Rights, this title focuses on the rights that the individual has as opposed to the rights of a society. The examination results in a categorization of the human rights of the declaration, which is compatible with the traditional distinction between political and civil rights and economic, social, and cultural rights.

Korey, William. **Human Rights and the Helsinki Accord: Focus on U.S. Policy** (Headline Series, no. 264). New York: Foreign Policy Association, 1983. 64p. $4. ISBN 0-87124-082-3. JC571 K67.

Korey relates how the Helsinki accord came into existence and traces it to 1983. The accord is so called because the first meeting of the Conference on Security and Cooperation in Europe was in Finlandia Hall in Helsinki. Includes discussion questions and reading list.

Lawyers Committee for Human Rights

See page 50 for a description of this organization. The following are book-length publications of the committee. Briefer reports are listed under its description in Chapter 4.

Crisis in Crossroads: A Report on Human Rights in South Africa. January 1988. 103p. $10.

This report focuses on the role of the South African government in the destruction of four squatter camps in the Crossroads area in Cape Province in May and June 1986, which left 51 dead, hundreds wounded, and 70,000 homeless. The account draws primarily from the affidavits and statements of residents, journalists, and clergy who witnessed the events. Analyzes the impact of continued vigilantism and forced removals on South Africa's black majority.

Critique: Review of the Department of State's Country Reports on Human Rights Practices for 1987. See Human Rights Watch.

Liberia, A Promise Betrayed: A Report on Human Rights. 1986. 176p. $10. ISBN 0-934143-13-7. JC599 L7 B47.

Written by Bill Berkeley, a journalist working as a consultant for the Lawyers Committee for Human Rights, this report is the result of a month-long fact-finding mission to Liberia in 1986 and subsequent research. It examines the country's continuing repression of political dissent and its excessive use of military force at a time of national upheaval. The report's conclusions are based primarily on eyewitness accounts presented by diverse and apparently credible sources. Whenever possible, corroborating documents and testimony were obtained.

The Persecution of Human Rights Monitors, December 1987 to December 1988: A Worldwide Survey. See Human Rights Watch.

The Reagan Administration's Record on Human Rights in 1988. See Human Rights Watch.

Seeking Shelter: Cambodians in Thailand: A Report on Human Rights. 1987. 114p.

The present title is based on an earlier report that investigated the status of human rights in Cambodia (now Kampuchea) six years after the Vietnamese invasion, which noted rumors of the mistreatment of Cambodians who fled to Thailand. Describes innumerable instances of torture and other types of mistreatment, not only by the Vietnamese troops along the border, but by the hordes of Cambodians, characterized as "bandits," that terrorize the camps.

The War against Children: South Africa's Youngest Victims. 1986. 151p. $10. ISBN 0-934143-00-5.

This report documents the detention, torture, and killing of black children by South Africa's apartheid government. Children, some as young as seven years old, have been held in solitary confinement, allegedly for being threats to state security; many have serious charges made against them, with little evidence, and if convicted, appear in court without any legal representation. Some of the government's violence against children has been brought on as a response to the protests voiced by student organizations.

Lillich, Richard B. **The Human Rights of Aliens in Contemporary International Law** (The Melland Schill Monographs in International Law). Dover, NH: Manchester University Press, 1984. 224p. $46. ISBN 0-7190-0914-6. K3274 L55.

This is a study by an international scholar-lawyer on the state of international law relating to the treatment of individual aliens from the perspective of human rights. Particular attention is given to the U.N. Draft Declaration on the Human Rights of Non-Citizens. Includes a copy of the document.

Macfarlane, L. J. **The Theory and Practice of Human Rights.** New York: St Martin's Press, 1985. 193p. $25. ISBN 0-312-79716-8. JC571 M2132.

In this examination of the principal characteristics of human rights, Macfarlane discusses what form selected key rights must take in order to be substantiated in universally applicable terms and explores the problems of implementing these rights.

McKean, Warwick. **Equality and Discrimination under International Law.** New York: Oxford University Press, 1983. 330p. $18.95. ISBN 0-19-825311-7. K3242 M35.

This major study of international documents and the decisions of international and municipal courts was undertaken to determine the extent to which there exist standards of international law concerning the equality of individuals. Includes an index of cases cited by various international and national groups.

Meron, Theodor, ed. **Human Rights in International Law: Legal and Policy Issues.** 2 vols. New York: Oxford University Press, 1984. ISBN 0-19-825472-5 (Vol. 1). ISBN 0-19-825488-1 (Vol. 2). K3240.4 H835.

Major legal scholars voice their views on political, economic, and social rights, including such topics as human rights in armed conflict, various regional protections, and race, sex, and religious discrimination.

Meron, Theodor. **Human Rights Law Making in the U.N.: A Critique of Instruments and Process.** New York: Oxford University Press, 1986. $22.50. 351p. ISBN 0-19-825549-7. K3240.4 M485.

The author attempts to demonstrate some of the weaknesses inherent in the U.N.'s methods of adapting human rights instruments and the resulting inadequacies of the instruments themselves. Three major documents are selected as examples: the International Convention on the Elimination of All Forms of Racial Discrimination, the Convention on the Elimination of All Forms of Discrimination against Women, and the International Covenant on Civil and Political Rights. Suggestions are made for the improvement of lawmaking techniques.

Milne, Alan J. M. **Human Rights and Human Diversity.** Albany, NY: State University of New York Press, 1986. 186p. $39.50. ISBN 0-88706-366-7. $12.95 (paper). ISBN 0-88706-367-5. K3240.4 M56.

This is a series of essays on the philosophy of human rights based on lectures and seminars the author gave over a period of seven years. The first part is devoted to essays on morality, and the second is on rights in general and human rights in particular. The final section covers human rights and politics.

Montgomery, John Warwick. **Human Rights and Human Dignity.** Dallas, TX: Probe Books, 1986. 319p. $14.95. ISBN 0-310-28571-2. JC571 M765.

The author, both a lawyer and a theologian, surveys existing human rights protections in international and domestic law and the role of governmental and nongovernmental organizations in the field. His examination of philosophical and theological implications concludes that the foundation for human rights must be found in the revelational context of the Bible. Contains the texts of some human rights instruments.

Mower, A. Glenn, Jr. **Human Rights and American Foreign Policy: The Carter and Reagan Experience** (Studies in Human Rights, no. 7). Westport, CT: Greenwood Press, 1987. 184p. $37.95. ISBN 0-313-25082-0. K3240.4 M675.

A general survey of the human rights policies of the Carter and Reagan administrations, this study deals with the conceptual framework within which each administration's policy was formed, the success of these policies, and the tactics for implementation. Includes case studies of South Africa and South Korea to illustrate the approach to human rights situations taken by the two administrations.

Mower, A. Glenn, Jr. **International Cooperation for Social Justice** (Studies in Human Rights, no. 6). Westport, CT: Greenwood Press, 1985. 271p. $35. ISBN 0-313-24702-1. K3240.4 M676.

The author addresses the topic of international protections for economic and social rights on the global level through an in-depth study of the U.N.'s International Covenant on Economic, Social and Cultural Rights and the European Social Charter, which originated in the Council of Europe.

Organization of American States (OAS). **Handbook of Existing Rules Pertaining to Human Rights in the Inter-American System.** Washington, DC: OAS, 1985. 201p. $8. ISBN 0-8270-2209-3.

This publication contains texts of the major human rights instruments relating to the member states of the OAS, e.g., the American Declaration of the Rights of Man, the American Convention on Human Rights, and the Regulations of the Inter-American Commission on Human Rights.

Also includes the texts of the instruments of ratification and a model statement form for individuals who wish to bring complaints regarding violations of human rights.

Organization of American States (OAS). **The Situation of Human Rights in Cuba.** Washington, DC: OAS, 1983. 183p. ISBN 0-8270-1883-5. JC599 C815.

This report is the product of an effort by the Inter-American Commission on Human Rights to evaluate the concrete results of the Cuban government's policies concerning human rights. It covers such topics as the right to a fair trial and to due process of law, the right to religious freedom, and worship, and the right to work.

Plattner, Marc F., ed. **Human Rights in Our Time: History, Theory, Policy.** Boulder, CO: Westview Press, 1984. 175p. $24.50. ISBN 0-86531-606-6. K3240.6 H877.

Collected in memory of Victor Baras, a young professor who as a teacher and expert on the Soviet bloc was devoted to human rights, these eight essays cover such topics as the philosophical foundation of human rights, affirmative action, and U.S. policy toward the Soviet Union.

Ramcharan, B. G. **Humanitarian Good Offices in International Law** (International Studies in Human Rights). The Hague: Martinus Nijhoff, 1983. Distributed by Kluwer Academic Publishers, Hingham, MA. 259p. $60.50. ISBN 90-247-2805-3. K3240.4 R35.

Delivered as the 1981 Reed Lecture at Acadia University, Wolfville, Nova Scotia, this text analyzes the concepts and characteristics of humanitarian good offices in international law with emphasis on the offices of the U.N.

Ramcharan, B. G., ed. **The Right to Life in International Law** (International Studies in Human Rights). The Hague: Martinus Nijhoff, 1985. Distributed by Kluwer Academic Publishers, Hingham, MA. 371p. $96.50. ISBN 90-247-3074-0. K3252 A55.

This volume presents essays by a distinguished group of scholars representing backgrounds in various political, economic, social, and legal systems on the complex problems relating to the right-to-life concept. Includes essays on the relationship between the right to life and the right to development, genocide and mass killings, and capital punishment.

Ray, Douglas, and Vincent D'Oyley, eds. **Human Rights in Canadian Education.** Dubuque, IA: Kendall/Hunt Publishing, 1983. 250p. $11.95. ISBN 0-8403-2983-0. LA412.7 H85.

Based on a conference on Human Rights in Canadian Education held at the Vancouver Theological College in 1979, this work considers three aspects of educational rights that are recognized internationally: (1) civil rights are safeguarded by tradition, legislation, and affirmation; (2) standards are set to ensure consistent policy; and (3) when a group has been victimized in the past, affirmative action may include educational advantages.

Reynaud, Alain. **Human Rights in Prisons.** Strasbourg: Council of Europe, Publications Section, 1986. ISBN 92-871-0881-1. K5514 R39.

Prepared at the request of the Committee of Experts for the Promotion of Education and Information in the Field of Human Rights of the Council of Europe, this guide is intended for prison directors and aims to highlight the human rights problems they are likely to encounter. The guide outlines relevant sections of human rights law, in part from the European Convention on Human Rights and its case law. Includes some comparisons of prison regulations of several European states.

Rhoodie, Eschel. **Discrimination in the Constitutions of the World: A Study of the Group Rights Problem.** Columbus, GA: Brentwood Communications Group, 1984. 461p. K3242 R46.

This is a study of group rights (as opposed to individual rights) relating to race, religion, ethnicity, and sex in 157 constitutions of the world. Almost a third of the volume is devoted to bibliography.

Scoble, Harry M., and Laurie S. Wiseberg, eds. **Access to Justice: The Struggle for Human Rights in South East Asia.** London: Zed Books, 1985. Distributed by Biblio Distribution Center, Totowa, NJ. 208p. $10.25. ISBN 0-86232-292-8. JC599 A8.

This publication is based on a workshop on access to justice held in the Philippines in February 1982. Sponsored by Human Rights Internet and the International Human Rights Law Group from the United States and the University of the Philippines College and Center for Law, the conference brought together some 40 participants from the Philippines, Indonesia, Thailand, and Malaysia, with a small group from the United States and India, to discuss various aspects of (1) Asian perspectives on human rights, (2) the present state of human rights in the Association of South East Asian Nations (ASEAN) region, and (3) particular rights and special programs.

Selby, David. **Human Rights** (Modern World Issues). New York: Cambridge University Press, 1987. 80p. ISBN 0-521-27419-2. JC571 S3917.

This title presents basic concepts about human rights from a British point of view. The first section discusses the nature of human rights, especially the differences in perception of human rights by East and West. The second section includes case studies relating to human rights in various parts of the world. The final section covers methods of defending human rights, particularly the role of the U.N., the European Convention on Human Rights, and Amnesty International.

Seymour, James D. **China Rights Annals 1: Human Rights Developments in the People's Republic of China from October 1983 through September 1984.** Armont, NY: M. E. Sharpe, 1985. 197p. $35. ISBN 0-87332-320-3. JC599 C6 S49.

The author attempts to bring together much of the current information about the status of human rights in the People's Republic of China at the time of writing. Part I analyzes internationally recognized human rights and the extent to which they are recognized in China; Part II analyzes the status of human rights in China from the Chinese perspective.

Shepherd, George W., and Ved P. Nanda, eds. **Human Rights and Third World Development** (Studies in Human Rights, no. 5). Westport, CT: Greenwood Press, 1985. 332p. $45. ISBN 0-313-24276-3. JC599 D44 H86.

This is a collection of studies by different authors that grew out of a seminar on human rights and development. Part I raises theoretical questions and sets the stage for Part II, which is devoted to case studies relating to Latin America, the People's Republic of China, the Middle East, and Africa. Part III explores the role of multinational corporations and the development of international nongovernmental organizations in protecting human rights.

Sigler, Jay A. **Minority Rights: A Comparative Analysis** (Contributions in Political Science, no. 104). Westport, CT: Greenwood Press, 1983. 245p. $32.95. ISBN 0-313-23400-0. K3242 S57.

Minority rights are not a high priority in most countries. The author discusses the main features of minority rights in order to promote an awareness of group rights in addition to the more familiar rights of individuals. Such topics as affirmative action and antidiscrimination policies are covered.

Skalnes, Tor, and Jan Egeland, eds. **Human Rights in Developing Countries, 1986: A Yearbook on Countries Receiving Norwegian Aid.** Oslo: Norwegian University Press, 1986. 312p. ISBN 82-00-18271-1. JC599 D44 H85.

Sponsored by the Norwegian government but carried out by independent researchers, this report examines human rights in ten countries: five in Africa, four in Asia and one in Central America. In addition to presenting information on human rights in each country, the Norwegian government helped to foster discussion on the criteria for selecting countries that should be given development aid. For each of the countries, information on the government, social indicators, civil and political rights, and ethnic, cultural, and religious minorities is given.

Stohl, Michael, and George A. Lopez, eds. **Government Violence and Repression: An Agenda for Research** (Contributions in Political Science, no. 148). Westport, CT: Greenwood Press, 1986. 278p. $35. ISBN 0-313-24651-3. JC571 G69.

Each author in this collection attempts to delineate a particular aspect of government violence in our time and to postulate how social science inquiry might proceed more systematically in the future. This group of scholars has set an agenda for the future of research to deal with these most extreme forms of government violence.

Swidler, Leonard, ed. **Religious Liberty and Human Rights in Nations and Religions.** Philadelphia: Ecumenical Press, Temple University, 1986. Copublished by Hippocrene Books. 255p. ISBN 0-931214-06-8. K3258 A55.

Scholars representing Buddhism, Christianity, Hinduism, Islam, and Judaism from 13 countries on four continents met to discuss religious liberty and human rights between nations, within nations, and within religions at a conference held at Temple University. This volume brings together the papers of the conference. Includes the Declaration on the Elimination of All Forms of Intolerance and of Discrimination Based on Religion or Belief, adopted by the U.N. General Assembly in November 1981.

Szymanski, Albert. **Human Rights in the Soviet Union.** London: Zed Books, 1984. Distributed by Biblio Distribution Center, Totowa, NJ. 338p. $30.95. ISBN 8-6232-018-6. JC599 R9.

A sociologist examines human rights in the Soviet Union and argues that the level of human rights there is considerably more advanced than is generally supposed in the West. He compares and contrasts human rights in the United States and the Soviet Union, including treatment of minorities, economic rights of the employed, and women's rights. Attempts to demythologize the human rights records of both superpowers.

Tarrow, Norma Bernstein, ed. **Human Rights and Education** (Comparative and International Education Series, vol.3). Elmsford, NY: Pergamon, 1987. 272p. $52. ISBN 0-08-03387-9. $26 (paper). ISBN 0-08-033415-6.

This collection gives an overview of the relationship between education and human rights—both the concept of education as a human right and education about human rights. Viewed in a comparative framework, the authors stress that education should lead to an understanding of and sympathy for the concepts of justice, democracy, peace, and responsibility. Includes discussion of teacher preparation for human rights education.

Tolley, Howard, Jr. **The U.N. Commission on Human Rights** (Westview Special Studies in International Relations). Boulder, CO: Westview Press; Frederick A. Praeger, Publisher, 1987. 300p. $35. ISBN 0-8133-7288-7. JC571 T66.

Tolley describes the historical development of the U.N. Commission on Human Rights from its beginnings in 1947 to 1986—from the drafting of the International Bill of Human Rights during 1947 to 1954, through the relatively inactive stages devoted primarily to research studies, to more recent periods characterized by heightened scrutiny of human rights violations in all regions of the world.

UNESCO. **Human Rights in Urban Areas.** Paris: UNESCO, 1983. 169p. $13.25. ISBN 92-3-101983-X. HT151 H85.

Based on an international symposium sponsored by Unesco in Paris in 1980, this volume explores the problems encountered in the implementation of human rights in urban areas. Contributors include not only jurists, sociologists, and other academics, but mayors, city planners, police chiefs, social workers, and others from all over the world who daily grapple with urban problems. It was the first such conference to explore these problems from the standpoint of human rights, and it stressed the necessity of promoting respect for human rights through training.

UNESCO. **Violations of Human Rights: Possible Rights of Recourse and Forms of Resistance.** Paris: UNESCO, 1984. 236p. $15.50. ISBN 92-3-102114-1. K3239.6.

This volume contains papers presented at a UNESCO meeting in Sierra Leone in 1981 that discussed the problems involved in the right to resist violations of human rights, tyranny, and other forms of injustice. While recognizing the right to resist, the authors suggest peaceful means of resistance, such as political and economic sanctions, as a better solution than armed conflict.

United Nations. **Human Rights: Questions and Answers.** New York: United Nations, 1987. 54p.

Prepared by the U.N. Department of Public Information, this booklet answers some of the questions often asked about the U.N. position with regard to human rights and their place in society. It examines some of the principal U.N. efforts to promote these rights. Includes a copy of the Universal Declaration of Human Rights.

United Nations. **U.N. Action in the Field of Human Rights.** New York: United Nations, 1988. 359p. $80. ISBN 92-1-154067-4. JC571 U3.

This is a detailed summary of human rights–related developments that have taken place within the U.N. system since its inception up to December 3, 1987. The book lists accomplishments in such areas as the rights of nations and peoples to self-determination, the advancement of women, the elimination of apartheid, and the protection of refugees, stateless persons, and vulnerable groups of persons. Essential for those working in international human rights issues.

U.S. Department of State. **Country Reports on Human Rights Practices for 1988.** Washington, DC: Government Printing Office, 1989. 1,570p. $33. ISBN 052-070-06535-4. JC571 C67.

This publication reports on human rights practices of all nations that receive U.S. foreign assistance as well as those that do not receive assistance but are members of the United Nations and those few nations that are not members of the United Nations. Reports on each country are based on various sources: nongovernmental organizations (NGOs), U.S. officials, officials of foreign countries, intelligence information, press reports, and individual victims of human rights violations. The reports are submitted to the Senate Committee on Foreign Relations and the House Committee on Foreign Affairs in accordance with specific sections of the Foreign Assistance Act of 1961. Includes chart of selected international human rights agreements.

Van Dyke, Vernon. **Human Rights, Ethnicity, and Discrimination** (Contributions in Ethnic Studies, no. 10). Westport, CT: Greenwood Press, 1985. 259p. $35. ISBN 0-313-24655-6. JC571 V26.

Van Dyke discusses the problems that arise when people of different cultures and goals interact. Frequently, one group dominates the others and there are violations of human rights. The author surveys the successful and unsuccessful remedies attempted by modern states to overcome those violations related to ethnicity.

Van Niekerk, Barend. **The Cloistered Virtue: Freedom of Speech and the Administration of Justice in the Western World.** New York: Praeger Publishers, 1987. 399p. $41.95. ISBN 0-275-92082-8. K3254 V36.

A widely traveled Afrikaner discusses legal free speech and how it has fared in the Western world. He examines the concept of freedom of speech, the formal restrictions on it, the problems of trial publicity restrictions, and informal restrictions. Concludes that legal free speech has been shortchanged far too often and that the struggle for freedom in this area, as in other human rights, must be pursued vigorously.

Veatch, Henry B. **Human Rights: Fact or Fiction?** Baton Rouge, LA: Louisiana State University Press, 1985. 258p. $30. ISBN 0-8071-1238-0. K3240.4 V42.

The author considers questions of ethics and political theory and attempts to synthesize traditional natural law theory. He sees natural rights as necessary conditions for human beings to meet their obligations to strive for self-development.

Verstappen, Berth, ed. **Human Rights Reports: An Annotated Bibliography of Fact-Finding Missions.** New York: Hans Zell Publishers for the Netherlands Institute of Human Rights, 1987. Distributed by K. G. Saur. 393p. $75. ISBN 0-905450-35-3. Z716 L6.

This bibliography brings together reports of fact-finding missions by both intergovernmental and nongovernmental organizations, covering the years 1970 to 1986. Reports deal with such human rights issues as religious freedom and the position of the churches, arrests, detentions and prison conditions, and refugees and displaced persons. Reports are arranged by continent and listed alphabetically by country or region.

Vincent, R. J. **Human Rights and International Relations.** New York: Cambridge University Press, 1986. Published in association with the Royal Institute of International Affairs. 194p. $34.50. ISBN 0-521-32798-9. $8.95 (paper). ISBN 0-521-33995-2. JC571 V554.

A discussion of the theory, practice, and policies of human rights. The first section deals with what human rights are, and the second, with what role they play in contemporary international politics. The third section attempts to answer the question, What ought to be done about human rights in international relations? Though human rights are treated as universal standards applicable to all foreign policy—not that of a specific country—the work is written from a Western point of view.

Welch, Claude E., and Ronald I. Meltzer, eds. **Human Rights and Development in Africa.** Albany, NY: State University of New York Press, 1984. 349p. $44.50. ISBN 0-87395-836-5. $17.95 (paper). ISBN 0-87395-837-3. JC599 A36 H84.

Although apartheid is discussed, the work purports to investigate less well known but perhaps more typical and highly significant human rights issues on the continent as a whole. A major purpose of the book is to clarify the connections between levels of development and local standards and practices of human rights. Each chapter is written by an expert in the field.

Wu, Yuan-li, et al. **Human Rights in the People's Republic of China.** Boulder, CO: Westview Press, 1988. 332p. $35. ISBN 0-8133-7439-1. JC599 C6 H86.

This is a joint undertaking by six authors who have devoted many years to research and writing on contemporary China. They review human rights in China from the inception of the PRC in 1949 until 1984. The authors cover general history, relationships between the state and the people, social bonds within families and communities, economic activities, culture, and thought processes—all of which have come under the continual assault and manipulation of the Communist party. The authors feel the story of the Chinese Communist experience, though changing, must be remembered as a part of the modern threat to human rights throughout the world.

Yarbrough, Tinsley E., ed. **The Reagan Administration and Human Rights.** New York: Praeger Publishers, 1985. 266p. $36.95. ISBN 0-275-90239-0. JC599 U5 R34.

These essays cover various aspects of human and civil rights during the Reagan administration and make some comparisons with the policies of the Carter administration. Some of the issues include gender discrimination, the ERA, voting rights, housing discrimination, affirmative action, and international human rights policies.

Periodicals

The following list includes those periodicals that have a strong human rights emphasis. Most are available in academic libraries and some can be found in local public libraries. Many articles on human rights can be found in other periodicals, however, and these can be accessed through standard indexes and abstracting journals. Those most useful for human rights issues are listed in the Reference Materials section.

Alberta Human Rights Journal
Alberta Human Rights Commission
10808 99th Avenue, Room 1006
Edmonton, Alberta, Canada T5K OG5
Quarterly. Free on request.

Although titled a journal, the format of this publication is more like that of a newsletter. Nonetheless, it has brief articles on human rights issues, particularly as they relate to the work of the Alberta Human Rights Commission, and it frequently describes cases of human rights complaints brought to the commission or human rights cases that come before the courts. A regular feature of the publication is Alberta Human Rights Update—"a newsletter for business and employers"—which deals with such issues as language in the workplace, a topic of interest to both employers and employees. Other features include letters to the editor and news items.

American Journal of International Law
American Society of International Law
2223 Massachusetts Avenue, NW
Washington, DC 20008
Quarterly. $50.

Sponsored by a society founded in 1906 "to foster the study of international law and to promote the establishment and maintenance of international relations on the basis of law and justice," this journal is one of the most authoritative and prestigious of the law journals. Published for its members, other lawyers, scholars, and jurists, it includes many articles on human rights issues. It also publishes book reviews and occasionally reprints treaties, conventions, and U.N. publications. It is indexed in law indexes and in general indexes such as *PAIS* and *Social Science Index.*

Bulletin of Human Rights
United Nations Division of Human Rights
Palais des Nations
1211 Geneva 10, Switzerland
Semiannual. Free.

Published in English, French, Russian, and Spanish, this publication carries information on the role of the United Nations in the promotion of human rights. It includes articles, copies of speeches given by U.N. officials, news of human rights events, reports of various commissions and committees relating to human rights, and book reviews. It ceased publication in 1982 but resumed in 1986.

Columbia Human Rights Law Review
Columbia University School of Law
435 West 116th Street, Box 25
New York, NY 10027
Semiannual. $18.

Formerly the *Columbia Survey of Human Rights Law* (1967–1968), this publication endeavors to illuminate subjects of concern regarding human rights, the law, and people's lives. It focuses on legal issues that are basic to all citizens, such as freedom of religion, freedom of speech, discrimination in employment, and women's rights, but does so more often from the viewpoint of the U.S. legal system rather than an international viewpoint. Contains book reviews. Indexed in *PAIS* and *Index to Legal Periodicals*.

Covert Action Information Bulletin (CAIB)
Covert Action Publications, Inc.
P.O. Box 50272
Washington, DC 20004
Quarterly. $22 (individuals, $17).

This quarterly covers the activities of the CIA and other intelligence agencies. Much of the information regarding these activities is difficult to find elsewhere. Many issues concentrate on one topic such as terrorism or disinformation campaigns. Contains occasional book and film reviews. Indexed in the *Alternative Press Index*.

Cultural Survival Quarterly
Cultural Survival, Inc.
11 Divinity Avenue
Cambridge, MA 02138
Quarterly. $20.

This journal addresses the immediate and long-term concerns of indigenous peoples throughout the world and attempts to raise public awareness regarding human rights abuses of indigenous peoples. Many of the issues are devoted to a single theme or topic, such as "Women in a Changing World." Also includes information about other groups interested in indigenous peoples and occasional book reviews and news items. Indexed in the *Alternative Press Index*.

Freedom at Issue
Freedom House
20 West 40th Street
New York, NY 10018
Bimonthly. $20.

Published by Freedom House, an organization dedicated to strengthening democratic institutions, each issue features several articles on such topics as religious freedom, land reform, and the effect of foreign policy on human rights. Also included are letters to the editor, news items, and fairly lengthy book reviews. Most of the content, both articles and news, focuses on Communist and Socialist countries. Indexed in *PAIS* and *Historical Abstracts*.

Human Rights
American Bar Association
Individual Rights and Responsibilities Section
750 North Lake Shore Drive
Chicago, IL 60611
Three issues per year. $18.

This periodical contains brief articles on such issues as refugees, children's rights, housing, gay and lesbian rights, and women in prison. More popular in style than most of the other human rights law publications, it includes news items and some book reviews. Indexed in several indexes, including *Social Science Index, Index to Legal Periodicals,* and *Legal Resource Index.*

Human Rights Bulletin
International League for Human Rights
432 Park Avenue South
New York, NY 10016
Semiannual. $20.

Formerly *Rights of Man,* the *Bulletin* appears in a newsletter format. It describes violations of human rights all over the world and gives a brief summary of cases that have already been noted by the League. It frequently requests readers to send appeals to authorities in specific cases. News of the League and its activities is also included.

Human Rights Internet (HRI) Reporter
Human Rights Internet
Harvard Law School
Pound Hall, Room 401
Cambridge, MA 02138
Quarterly. $60 (individuals, $40).

The *HRI Reporter* is intended to help keep the human rights community informed about major international and national developments as they affect human rights worldwide. It seeks to spotlight nongovernmental organizations (NGOs) working for the protection and promotion of human rights; focus attention on human rights defenders under attack; review important decisions and actions of intergovernmental organizations and governmental bodies with a human rights mandate; stimulate discussion, research, and teaching in the field of human rights; and assist human rights advocacy organizations and policymakers. The journal is now divided into three main sections: the first includes editorial comments, brief articles by outside contributors, and a calendar; the second includes information on developments of importance to the human rights community, including the work of the U.N.; and the third is the bibliography section—lists of fairly lengthy descriptions of human rights literature from all over the world, arranged primarily by geographic region. Material in the bibliography is indexed by geographic region, by subject, and by organization. In the first issue of each volume, a master list of organizations is published, with updates included in the following issues. The *HRI Reporter* is without doubt the most valuable tool for those interested in human rights; it is probably the most thorough and accurate serial publication in the field of human rights in the world.

Human Rights Law Journal
N. P. Engel, Publisher
3608 South 12th Street
Arlington, VA 22204
Quarterly. $64.

A forum for scholarly debate in the field of human rights law, the *Journal* endeavors to serve as a channel of communication between both sides of the Atlantic. Formerly the *Human Rights Law Review,* it is published in association with the International Institute of Human Rights in Strasbourg and reports on constitutional and supreme court decisions in the human rights field from all over Europe. Indexed in *Index to Legal Periodicals* and *Legal Resource Index.*

Human Rights Quarterly
Johns Hopkins University Press
Journals Publishing Division
701 West 40th Street, Suite 275
Baltimore, MD 21211
Quarterly. $54 (individuals, $19.50).

Tied to no particular ideology, the *Human Rights Quarterly* offers scholars in the fields of philosophy, law, and the social sciences an interdisciplinary forum in which to present comparative and international research on public policy within the scope of the Universal Declaration of Human Rights. Each issue contains scholarly, well-documented articles and book reviews. The journal is sponsored by the Urban Morgan Institute for Human Rights, College of Law, at the University of Cincinnati. Indexed in *PAIS, the Philosopher's Index,* and *Legal Resource Index.*

Index on Censorship
Writers and Scholars International, Ltd.
39c Highbury Place
London N5 1QP, England
Ten issues per year. $27.50.

A British publication with supporters in many countries, including the Fund for Free Expression in the United States, the *Index on Censorship* attempts to raise awareness of such issues as freedom of the press, academic freedom, and freedom of creative expression. The several articles in each issue reflect this purpose. Also included are "News and Notes," book reviews, and "Index, Index"—a country-by-country account of censorship and other violations of human rights, such as the killing of a human rights lawyer in Haiti. Indexed in *PAIS* and the *Alternative Press Index*.

New York Law School Journal of Human Rights
New York Law School
57 Worth Street
New York, NY 10013-2960
Semiannual. $18.

Changed from *New York Law School Human Rights Annual* to its present title in 1987, the journal is dedicated to the international protection of human rights. Though some are more properly concerned with civil rights, generally the articles—which are scholarly and well documented—deal with basic human rights. Some of the issues treated are children's rights, the rights of the mentally disabled, the Sanctuary Movement, and homelessness. Indexed in *PAIS* and the *Index to Legal Periodicals*.

Third World Resources: A Quarterly Review of Resources from and about the Third World
Third World Resources
464 19th Street
Oakland, CA 94612
Quarterly. $25 (individuals, $25 for two years).

Published to alert educators, activists, and others to resources related to Third World regions and problems, each issue has sections on organizations, books, periodicals, pamphlets and articles, and audiovisuals. Almost all are related to human rights issues and many are resources that are not easily found elsewhere. Materials are generally given fairly lengthy reviews along with bibliographic information. Feature Inserts provide materials on one region—a recent one was on the Philippines— or on a theme. Very useful for anyone interested in human rights in the Third World.

WIN News
187 Grant Street
Lexington, MA 02173
Quarterly. $40 (individuals, $30).

WIN (Women's International Network) News is "a worldwide open communication system by, for, and about women of all backgrounds, beliefs, nationalities, and age groups." Though not strictly a human rights journal, most of the articles are on the basic rights of women from an international perspective. Some of the articles in recent issues cover legal rights of women in countries like Pakistan and Japan, equality in education and employment, repressive religious groups and women's rights, and women and work.

6

Nonprint Media, Computer Networks, and Databases

Nonprint Media

There are few nonprint materials on human rights as such, but there are many on human rights issues such as hunger, imprisonment and torture, disappearances and political killings, refugees, the rights of women, and labor rights. One of the few sources for information specifically on human rights is the *Human Rights Film Guide,* edited by Anne Gelman and Milos Stehlik in 1985 (see the Reference Materials section in Chapter 5). The following are selected films, audio and videotapes that exemplify the types of nonprint materials available. Included at the end is a list of some of the distributors of nonprint materials aimed at raising public awareness of human rights issues.

Films and Videocassettes

Danylo Shumuk: Life Sentence
Type: Color Videocassette (VHS)
Length: 27 min.
Cost: Rental $20
Date: 1987

Distributor: Amnesty International
                 322 Eighth Avenue
                 New York, NY 10001
                 (212) 807-8400

Jailed by the Poles, Nazis, and Soviets, Danylo Shumuk spent more than 42 years in detention for the nonviolent expression of his political opinions. Depicts his life and story and how Amnesty International's efforts sustained him during his imprisonment.

The Dark Light of Dawn

Type:	Color videocassette (VHS/Beta)
Length:	28 min.
Cost:	Purchase $50
Date:	1987
Distributor:	Guatemala Human Rights Commission/USA
	P.O. Box 91, Cardinal Station
	Washington, DC 20064
	(202) 529-6599

An award-winning video documentary on the *Grupo de Apoyo* (Mutual Support Group) searching for "disappeared" relatives in Guatemala. Includes the plight of the Indians, reeducation camps, and "model villages," and the continuing suffering of the rural Indian population and other Guatemalans who are trying to end violations of human rights in their country.

Dateline: San Salvador

Type:	Color videocassette
Length:	28 min.
Cost:	Rental $35, purchase $70 (community groups and individuals); rental $50, apply for purchase price (institutions and libraries)
Date:	1986
Distributor:	Media Action Group
	P.O. Box 291575
	Los Angeles, CA 90029
	(213) 461-7305

Documents the historic march of Salvadorans through the streets of their capital to demand an end to the seven-year-old-civil war and to the years of government repression. Features a walking tour through the ruins of the national university, a visit to a refugee camp, and a look at a sack factory where workers are battling for their union and their own survival. Includes interviews with Salvadoran human rights and labor activists.

Don't Eat Today, or Tomorrow

Type:	16mm color film or videotape
Length:	43 min.
Cost:	Rental $85; purchase $695 (film), $420 (video)
Date:	1985
Distributor:	First Run/Icarus Films
	200 Park Avenue South, Suite 1319
	New York, NY 10003
	(212) 674-3375

During the recent period of military dictatorship in Argentina some 30,000 people "disappeared." After the disastrous Falkland Islands War, the country "conceded" to democracy, but with a $50 billion national debt. This film clarifies the relationship between the economic policies of the military and its acts of repression. It also looks at the role of multinational banks and corporations and the International Monetary Fund.

Genocide

Type:	16mm color film
Length:	52 min.
Cost:	Rental $75
Distributor:	Anti-Defamation League of B'nai B'rith
	Dept. JW
	823 United Nations Plaza
	New York, NY 10017
	(212) 490-2525

A documentary that tells the story of Hitler's "final solution." Set within an historic frame—from the 1920s when a wave of anti-Semitism swept through Germany to 1945 when the remnants of European Jewry were released from the death camps—the film exposes the methodical insanity of the Nazi era. Includes interviews with death camp survivors as well as with Germans who were directly involved in implementing the "final solution." Produced by Thames Television as part of The World at War series, narrated by Laurence Olivier.

International Human Rights

Type:	Color videocassette (VHS)
Length:	60 min.
Cost:	Purchase $59
Date:	1986
Distributor:	Zenger Video
	10200 Jefferson Boulevard, Room VC4
	P.O. Box 802
	Culver City, CA 90232-0802
	(800) 421-4246; (213) 839-2436 in CA

John G. Healey, executive director of Amnesty International USA, answers questions about the state of human rights in general and the work of Amnesty in particular. He describes the organization's work in pressuring governments into correcting human rights violations by bringing abuses to public attention. He also explains what types of human rights violations Amnesty monitors, how it collects information, and how it campaigns for improvements in human rights conditions.

Maids and Madams

Type:	Color videocassette (VHS)
Length:	52 min.
Cost:	Purchase $195
Date:	1985
Distributor:	Filmmakers Library
	124 East 40th Street
	New York, NY 10016
	(212) 808-4980

Shows the tragedy of apartheid in South Africa through the depiction of relationships between black women who work as maids and their female employers. The black women must leave their own children in the "homelands" in order to raise the children of the white women. The film also shows the influence of the Black Sash, the Domestic Workers Association, and other groups seeking to redress the injustices these black women suffer.

The Prejudice Film

Type:	Color videocassette (VHS)
Length:	28 min.
Cost:	Purchase $80
Distributor:	Social Studies School Service
	10200 Jefferson Boulevard, Room 15
	P.O. Box 802
	Culver City, CA 90232-9983
	(800) 421-4246; (213) 839-2436 in CA

Narrated by David Hartman, this film examines the historical origins and contemporary patterns of prejudice through a series of vignettes depicting various types of prejudice. It discusses the many manifestations of prejudice, from the innocent telling of an ethnic joke through acts of violence. The film raises questions of the individual's role in perpetuating or eradicating attitudes that result in discrimination against racial, ethnic, and religious groups.

Roots of Hunger; Roots of Change

Type:	16mm color film
Length:	27 min.

Cost: Rental $15
Date: 1985
Distributor: EcuFilm
              810 Twelfth Avenue, South
              Nashville, TN 37203
              (800) 251-4091; (615) 242-6277 in TN

Produced by Church World Service, this film examines the problem of hunger in Senegal, looking at its historical causes and their impact on people today. It documents the negative effect of cash cropping, a lingering vestige of the French colonial period, and examines a model of community development in which Church World Service has worked in partnership with the people to help them grow their own food and take control of their lives. An insightful look at a problem common not only in Africa but in many regions of the world.

Sanctuary
Type: 16mm color film or videotape
Length: 59 min.
Cost: Rental $100; purchase $895 (film), $540 (video)
Date: 1984
Distributor: First Run/Icarus Films
              200 Park Avenue South, Suite 1319
              New York, NY 10003
              (212) 674-3375

Filmed in Central America, Africa, the Middle East, and the United States, *Sanctuary* is a dramatic film on the world's refugee crisis. The story of one refugee family caught up in a civil war and forced to flee their homeland, it is enacted by five different families from different parts of the world. The last event leads to a heated debate on the politics of the sanctuary movement and the role of the church community in it.

The Trial in Gdansk
Type: ٭   Videocassette
Length: 50 min.
Cost: Rental $20
Distributor: Center for the Study of Human Rights
              Columbia University
              420 West 118th Street
              New York, NY 10027
              (212) 280-2479

Shows a rare glimpse into human rights abuses, political persecution, and corrupt courtroom practices in Poland. This student-acted/directed video is based on actual recordings smuggled to the United States from Poland. It recreates the dramatic episodes of the secret 1985 trial of three Solidarity members, including the well-known Adam Michnik.

The Twice Discriminated

Type:	Color Videocassette
Length:	86 min.
Cost:	Rental $70
Date:	1986
Distributor:	B. Kailasam
	716 East Burlington, #9
	Iowa City, IA 52240
	(319) 338-2669

Based on conversations with a cross-section of people in South India, this film explores the problems of caste, untouchability, and religious discrimination in India. Shows the background of untouchability and how it has come from Hinduism into the Indian Christian community and to other minority religions. The film is built around the conversations the film producer had with untouchable citizens and other Hindus and Christians (in subtitles) and is interspersed with commentary on government policies and historical background.

Voices of the Voiceless

Type:	Color Videocassette (VHS or Beta)
Length:	58 min.
Cost:	Rental $35 (½″), $50 (¾″); purchase $45 (½″), $125 (¾″)
Date:	1987
Distributor:	The Educational Film & Video Project
	1529 Josephine Street
	Berkeley, CA 94703
	(415) 849-1649

Depicts the half million El Salvadoran refugees and the U.S.-supported war that drove them to flee their country and live in the United States, many illegally. Filmed in El Salvador and in the Los Angeles refugee community, this film raises questions not only about the brutal repression the refugees suffered in their own country, but about the constant fear of deportation they must live with while in the United States, and whether this is humane treatment.

Voyage of Dreams

Type:	16mm color film or videotape
Date:	1983
Cost:	Rental $50; purchase $425 (film), $295 (video)
Length:	30 min.
Distributor:	Cinema Guild
	1697 Broadway
	New York, NY 10019
	(212) 246-5522

Coproduced by Haitian and Afro-American artists, this film describes the Haitian boat people and raises questions about the conditions in Haiti that forced them to flee and about U.S relations with this country, which is the poorest in the Western Hemisphere. Makes use of computer-generated art to illustrate some of the issues.

Filmstrips and Audio Tapes

Acts of Hate
Type: Radio broadcast on cassette tape
Length: 60 min.
Cost: Purchase $5
Date: 1988
Distributor: Radio Project California Tomorrow
849 South Broadway, Suite 831
Los Angeles, CA 90014
(213) 623-6231

This program, presented by California Tomorrow, is a documentary that focuses on racial, ethnic, religious, and minority tensions and on vandalism and violence in California.

Human Rights
Type: Color filmstrip with cassette
Cost: Purchase $37
Date: 1988
Distributor: Social Studies School Service
10200 Jefferson Boulevard, Room 15
P.O. Box 802
Culver City, CA 90232-0802
(800) 421-4246; (213) 839-2436 in CA

Dramatic portraits of what repressive governments can do to the human spirit highlight this program which places human rights in a global perspective. Compares human rights with the basic liberties guaranteed in Magna Carta, the Declaration of Independence, and the Universal Declaration of Human Rights. Designed as a teaching tool to help students understand how the United States can help eliminate human rights violations around the world.

Networking against Female Sexual Slavery
Type: Cassette tape
Length: 38 min.
Cost: Purchase $11

Date: 1984
Distributor: Pacifica Radio Archives
               5316 Venice Boulevard
               Los Angeles, CA 90019
               (213) 931-1625

Charlotte Bunch, a feminist theorist, discusses the nature and extent of female sexual slavery, a worldwide problem that is related to women's economic exploitation. Some nations consider poor women's bodies to be one of their prime resources for improving their economies.

World Hunger: What's the Solution?
Type: Color filmstrip with cassette
Cost: Purchase $32
Date: 1985
Distributor: Social Studies School Service
               10200 Jefferson Boulevard, Room 15
               P.O. Box 82
               Culver City, CA 90232-0802
               (800) 421-4246; (213) 839-2436 in CA

Introduces the viewer to the tragedy of famine and malnutrition in Ethiopia, other parts of Africa, and less publicized areas of the world. Discusses the role of the United Nations and the World Council of Churches and various programs industrialized nations can adopt to alleviate or prevent the problem of hunger in the future.

In addition to the distributors listed for the materials above, the following is a selected list of distributors who also have human rights–related nonprint materials.

Alternative Media Information
  Center
121 Fulton Street, 5th Floor
New York, NY 10038
(212) 619-3455

American Friends Service
  Committee
1501 Cherry Street
Philadelphia, PA 19102
(215) 241-7000

Asia Resource Center
P.O. Box 15275
Washington, DC 20003

(202) 547-1114
California Newsreel
630 Natoma Street
San Francisco, CA 94103
(415) 621-6196

Cambridge Documentary Films
P.O. Box 385
Cambridge, MA 02139
(617) 354-3677

Camino Film Project
P.O. Box 291575
Los Angeles, CA 90029
(213) 461-7305

Carousel Films, Inc.
241 East 34th Street, Room 304
New York, NY 10016
(212) 683-1660

Church World Service
28606 Phillips Street
P.O. Box 968
Elkhart, IN 46515
(219) 264-3102

Development Education Centre
229 College Street
Toronto, Ontario
Canada M5T 1R4
(416) 597-0524

Direct Cinema Limited
P.O. Box 69799
Los Angeles, CA 90069
(213) 652-8000

Franciscan Communications
1229 Santee Street
Los Angeles, CA 90015
(213) 746-2916

Great Atlantic Radio Conspiracy
2743 Maryland Avenue
Baltimore, MD 21218

IDERA Films
2524 Cypress Street
Vancouver, British Columbia
Canada V6J 3N2
(604) 738-8815

Ladyslipper (for audio
  resources)
P.O. Box 3124
Durham, NC 27705
(919) 683-1570

Lutheran World Ministries
  Media
10466 Plano Road
Dallas, TX 75238
(800) 527-3211

Maryknoll World Films
Maryknoll, NY 10545
(800) 258-5838; (914) 941-7687
  in NY

Mennonite Central Committee
21 South Street
Akron, PA 17501
(717) 859-1151

Media Guild
11722 Sorrento Valley Road,
  Suite E
San Diego, CA 92121
(619) 755-9191

Redwood Records
6400 Hollis Street
Emeryville, CA 94608
(415) 428-9191

Southern Africa Media Center
630 Natoma Street
San Francisco, CA 94103
(416) 621-6196

Third World Newsreel
160 Fifth Avenue, Suite 911
New York, NY 10010
(212) 243-2310

Wombat Film and Video
250 West 57th Street, Suite 916
New York, NY 10019
(212) 315-2502

Women's International News
  Gathering Service
P.O. Box 6758
San Francisco, CA 94101

World Council of Churches
U.S. Office
475 Riverside Drive, Room 1062
New York, NY 10115
(212) 870-2533

Computer Networks

This section includes general computer information services that link users with indexes and abstracts leading to specific human rights materials and a more specialized network. The first three included here are the more popular services available in many libraries and organizations; the fourth focuses on human rights, peace, and environmental issues.

BRS Information Technologies
1200 Route 9
Latham, NY 12110
(800) 833-4707; (800) 553-5561 in NY

BRS includes the following: Legal Resource Index, Magazine Index, PAIS International, Religion Index.

DIALOG Information Services
3460 Hillview Avenue
Palo Alto, CA 94304
(800) 3-DIALOG

DIALOG includes the following: A-V Online, Historical Abstracts, Legal Resource Index, PAIS International, Religion Index.

Wilsonline
H. W. Wilson Co.
950 University Avenue
Bronx, NY 10452
(800) 367-6770

The H. W. Wilson Company, a long-time publisher of reference materials, provides the following indexes online: Index to Legal Periodicals, Readers' Guide to Periodical Literature, Social Science Index.

PeaceNet
3228 Sacramento Street
San Francisco, CA 94115
(415) 923-0900

PeaceNet is a communications network that has several facets. The software provides for electronic mail, conferencing, access to specialized databases, and many other activities. Some human rights groups use PeaceNet to communicate with their members, to inform others about legislation or events, or to seek assistance. Amnesty International, for example, uses the network for its Urgent Action Alerts, which give information regarding prisoners of conscience who are under threat of torture or death to those willing to write letters or send telegrams to government authorities around the world on behalf of these prisoners. The bibliographical materials in *Third World Resources* are now available through the network. Since PeaceNet is relatively inexpensive, it is possible for many small groups and also individuals to participate in its services.

Databases

The following organizations have computer databases useful for human rights researchers or activists, but they are not available online to the public:

Human Rights Internet (HRI), described in Chapter 4, has established several computerized databases containing all the citations and articles found in the *HRI Reporter*. The databases also contain information on the human rights organizations around the world, which is frequently updated in the *Reporter*. Persons wishing to access this information can call or write HRI with their request and the staff will design a search and provide an annotated bibliography of citations. Copies of original documents can usually be provided also if they are not readily available elsewhere. Charges are based on the nature of the search, document reproduction, and staff assistance required.

Third World Resources (see Chapter 4) also has a computer-accessible database on Third World organizations and materials, most of which are human rights–related, based on research gathered for the Third World Resources directories and the quarterly publication, *Third World Resources* (see the Periodicals section in Chapter 5). Since it is an affiliate of the Data Center, an information service providing information for the public interest community, and is located in the same quarters, it is possible to have a search done that would cover materials of both groups. Call or write Third World Resources for costs.

7

Selected Human Rights Instruments

AS A PART OF THE ACTIVITIES carried out to commemorate the fortieth anniversary of the Universal Declaration of Human Rights, the U.N. Centre for Human Rights in Geneva published the fifth edition of a compilation of human rights instruments, titled *Human Rights: A Compilation of International Instruments,* that includes instruments adopted up through 1987. On the following pages appears a selection of these documents.

The U.N. compilation of these instruments covers some 15 categories, including almost all areas of the human condition, from slavery and forced labor to the right to enjoy culture. It is, therefore, difficult to make a selection from them that would suit the needs and interests of various readers. Since this work is intended primarily for American users, the instruments selected are for the most part those that might be of particular interest to the American public.

No selection of human rights instruments would be adequate without the Universal Declaration of Human Rights and its covenants, known collectively as the International Bill of Human Rights, since they form the basis for all the other instruments. They are, therefore, included first, followed by the International Convention on the Elimination of All Forms of Racial Discrimination, for somewhat the same reason. One might argue that racial discrimination is the basis for many of the world's problems, and though the United States has made great strides in this area, racial discrimination persists in various forms.

The Convention on Genocide is included because only recently was it ratified by the United States. Many have long advocated its ratification and wonder why it took 40 years for the United States to adopt this instrument.

The instrument relating to prisoners seems appropriate to include since U.S. prisons are filling up faster than they can be built. The resulting overcrowded and sometimes inhumane penal conditions have in a few instances prompted the courts to order prisons to reduce their populations or be shut down. A nation's citizens must either pay for more prisons or support those who believe there are alternatives to incarceration for at least some of the prison population.

The Convention on Freedom of Association seems relevant in view of recent media accounts of government spying on groups known to oppose government policy. The final instruments relate to the care a society is obliged to give those who frequently are unable to defend their rights—children, the mentally retarded, and the disabled. Only recently have some of the violations of the rights of persons in these groups been made public. These instruments serve to remind us of the responsibilities governments and individuals have in this area.

The International Bill of Human Rights

Universal Declaration of Human Rights

Adopted and proclaimed by General Assembly resolution 217 A (III)
of 10 December 1948

PREAMBLE

Whereas recognition of the inherent dignity and of the equal and inalienable rights of all members of the human family is the foundation of freedom, justice and peace in the world,

Whereas disregard and contempt for human rights have resulted in barbarous acts which have outraged the conscience of mankind, and the advent of a world in which human beings shall enjoy freedom of speech and belief and freedom from fear and want has been proclaimed as the highest aspiration of the common people,

Whereas it is essential, if man is not to be compelled to have recourse, as a last resort, to rebellion against tyranny and oppression, that human rights should be protected by the rule of law,

Whereas it is essential to promote the development of friendly relations between nations,

Whereas the peoples of the United Nations have in the Charter reaffirmed their faith in fundamental human rights, in the dignity and worth of the human person and in the equal rights of men and women and have determined to promote social progress and better standards of life in larger freedom,

Whereas Member States have pledged themselves to achieve, in cooperation with the United Nations, the promotion of universal respect for and observance of human rights and fundamental freedoms,

Whereas a common understanding of these rights and freedoms is of the greatest importance for the full realization of this pledge,

Now, therefore,

The General Assembly,

Proclaims this Universal Declaration of Human Rights as a common standard of achievement for all peoples and all nations, to the end that every individual and every organ of society, keeping this Declaration constantly in mind, shall strive by teaching and education to promote respect for these rights and freedoms and by progressive measures, national and international, to secure their universal and effective recognition and observance, both among the peoples of Member States themselves and among the peoples of territories under their jurisdiction.

Article 1

All human beings are born free and equal in dignity and rights. They are endowed with reason and conscience and should act towards one another in a spirit of brotherhood.

Article 2

Everyone is entitled to all the rights and freedoms set forth in this Declaration, without distinction of any kind, such as race, colour, sex, language, religion, political or other opinion, national or social origin, property, birth or other status.

Furthermore, no distinction shall be made on the basis of the political, jurisdictional or international status of the country or territory to which a person belongs, whether it be independent, trust, non-self-governing or under any other limitation of sovereignty.

Article 3

Everyone has the right to life, liberty and security of person.

Article 4

No one shall be held in slavery or servitude; slavery and the slave trade shall be prohibited in all their forms.

Article 5

No one shall be subjected to torture or to cruel, inhuman or degrading treatment or punishment.

Article 6

Everyone has the right to recognition everywhere as a person before the law.

Article 7

All are equal before the law and are entitled without any discrimination to equal protection of the law. All are entitled to equal protection against any discrimination in violation of this Declaration and against any incitement to such discrimination.

Article 8

Everyone has the right to an effective remedy by the competent national tribunals for acts violating the fundamental rights granted him by the constitution or by law.

Article 9

No one shall be subjected to arbitrary arrest, detention or exile.

Article 10

Everyone is entitled in full equality to a fair and public hearing by an independent and impartial tribunal, in the determination of his rights and obligations and of any criminal charge against him.

Article 11

1.   Everyone charged with a penal offence has the right to be presumed innocent until proved guilty according to law in a public trial at which he has had all the guarantees necessary for his defence.

2.   No one shall be held guilty of any penal offence on account of any act or omission which did not constitute a penal offence, under national or international law, at the time when it was committed. Nor shall a heavier penalty be imposed than the one that was applicable at the time the penal offence was committed.

Article 12

No one shall be subjected to arbitrary interference with his privacy, family, home or correspondence, nor to attacks upon his honour and reputation. Everyone has the right to the protection of the law against such interference or attacks.

Article 13

1.   Everyone has the right to freedom of movement and residence within the borders of each State.

2.   Everyone has the right to leave any country, including his own, and to return to his country.

Article 14

1.   Everyone has the right to seek and to enjoy in other countries asylum from persecution.

2.   This right may not be invoked in the case of prosecutions genuinely arising from non-political crimes or from acts contrary to the purposes and principles of the United Nations.

Article 15

1.   Everyone has the right to a nationality.

2.   No one shall be arbitrarily deprived of his nationality nor denied the right to change his nationality.

Article 16

1.   Men and women of full age, without any limitation due to race, nationality or religion, have the right to marry and to found a family. They are entitled to equal rights as to marriage, during marriage and at its dissolution.

2.   Marriage shall be entered into only with the free and full consent of the intending spouses.

3.   The family is the natural and fundamental group unit of society and is entitled to protection by society and the State.

Article 17

1.   Everyone has the right to own property alone as well as in association with others.

2.   No one shall be arbitrarily deprived of his property.

Article 18

Everyone has the right to freedom of thought, conscience and religion; this right includes freedom to change his religion or belief, and freedom, either alone or in community with others and in public or private, to manifest his religion or belief in teaching, practice, worship and observance.

Article 19

Everyone has the right to freedom of opinion and expression; this right includes freedom to hold opinions without interference and to seek, receive and impart information and ideas through any media and regardless of frontiers.

Article 20

1.   Everyone has the right to freedom of peaceful assembly and association.

2.   No one may be compelled to belong to an association.

Article 21

1.   Everyone has the right to take part in the government of his country, directly or through freely chosen representatives.

2.   Everyone has the right to equal access to public service in his country.

3. The will of the people shall be the basis of the authority of government: this will shall be expressed in periodic and genuine elections which shall be by universal and equal suffrage and shall be held by secret vote or by equivalent free voting procedures.

Article 22

Everyone, as a member of society, has the right to social security and is entitled to realization, through national effort and international co-operation and in accordance with the organization and resources of each State, of the economic, social and cultural rights indispensable for his dignity and the free development of his personality.

Article 23

1. Everyone has the right to work, to free choice of employment, to just and favourable conditions of work and to protection against unemployment.

2. Everyone, without any discrimination, has the right to equal pay for equal work.

3. Everyone who works has the right to just and favourable remuneration ensuring for himself and his family an existence worthy of human dignity, and supplemented, if necessary, by other means of social protection.

4. Everyone has the right to form and to join trade unions for the protection of his interests.

Article 24

Everyone has the right to rest and leisure, including reasonable limitation of working hours and periodic holidays with pay.

Article 25

1. Everyone has the right to a standard of living adequate for the health and well-being of himself and of his family, including food, clothing, housing and medical care and necessary social services, and the right to security in the event of unemployment, sickness, disability, widowhood, old age or other lack of livelihood in circumstances beyond his control.

2. Motherhood and childhood are entitled to special care and assistance. All children, whether born in or out of wedlock, shall enjoy the same social protection.

Article 26

1. Everyone has the right to education. Education shall be free, at least in the elementary and fundamental stages. Elementary education shall be compulsory. Technical and professional education shall be made generally

available and higher education shall be equally accessible to all on the basis of merit.

2.   Education shall be directed to the full development of the human personality and to the strengthening of respect for human rights and fundamental freedoms. It shall promote understanding, tolerance and friendship among all nations, racial or religious groups, and shall further the activities of the United Nations for the maintenance of peace.

3.   Parents have a prior right to choose the kind of education that shall be given to their children.

Article 27

1.   Everyone has the right freely to participate in the cultural life of the community, to enjoy the arts and to share in scientific advancement and its benefits.

2.   Everyone has the right to the protection of the moral and material interests resulting from any scientific, literary or artistic production of which he is the author.

Article 28

Everyone is entitled to a social and international order in which the rights and freedoms set forth in this Declaration can be fully realized.

Article 29

1.   Everyone has duties to the community in which alone the free and full development of his personality is possible.

2.   In the exercise of his rights and freedoms, everyone shall be subject only to such limitations as are determined by law solely for the purpose of securing due recognition and respect for the rights and freedoms of others and of meeting the just requirements of morality, public order and the general welfare in a democratic society.

3.   These rights and freedoms may in no case be exercised contrary to the purposes and principles of the United Nations.

Article 30

Nothing in this Declaration may be interpreted as implying for any State, group or person any right to engage in any activity or to perform any act aimed at the destruction of any of the rights and freedoms set forth herein.

International Covenant on Economic, Social and Cultural Rights

*Adopted and opened for signature, ratification and accession by General Assembly
resolution 2200 A (XXI) of 16 December 1966*

ENTRY INTO FORCE: 3 January 1976, in accordance with article 27

PREAMBLE

The States Parties to the present Covenant,

Considering that, in accordance with the principles proclaimed in the Charter of the United Nations, recognition of the inherent dignity and of the equal and inalienable rights of all members of the human family is the foundation of freedom, justice and peace in the world,

Recognizing that these rights derive from the inherent dignity of the human person,

Recognizing that, in accordance with the Universal Declaration of Human Rights, the ideal of free human beings enjoying freedom from fear and want can only be achieved if conditions are created whereby everyone may enjoy his economic, social and cultural rights, as well as his civil and political rights,

Considering the obligation of States under the Charter of the United Nations to promote universal respect for, and observance of, human rights and freedoms,

Realizing that the individual, having duties to other individuals and to the community to which he belongs, is under a responsibility to strive for the promotion and observance of the rights recognized in the present Covenant,

Agree upon the following articles:

PART I

Article 1

1. All peoples have the right of self-determination. By virtue of that right they freely determine their political status and freely pursue their economic, social and cultural development.

2. All peoples may, for their own ends, freely dispose of their natural wealth and resources without prejudice to any obligations arising out of international economic co-operation, based upon the principle of mutual benefit, and international law. In no case may a people be deprived of its own means of subsistence.

3.   The States Parties to the present Covenant, including those having responsibility for the administration of Non-Self-Governing and Trust Territories, shall promote the realization of the right of self-determination, and shall respect that right, in conformity with the provisions of the Charter of the United Nations.

PART II

Article 2

1.   Each State Party to the present Covenant undertakes to take steps, individually and through international assistance and co-operation, especially economic and technical, to the maximum of its available resources, with a view to achieving progressively the full realization of the rights recognized in the present Covenant by all appropriate means, including particularly the adoption of legislative measures.

2.   The States Parties to the present Covenant undertake to guarantee that the rights enunciated in the present Covenant will be exercised without discrimination of any kind as to race, colour, sex, language, religion, political or other opinion, national or social origin, property, birth or other status.

3.   Developing countries, with due regard to human rights and their national economy, may determine to what extent they would guarantee the economic rights recognized in the present Covenant to non-nationals.

Article 3

The States Parties to the present Covenant undertake to ensure the equal right of men and women to the enjoyment of all economic, social and cultural rights set forth in the present Covenant.

Article 4

The States Parties to the present Covenant recognize that, in the enjoyment of those rights provided by the State in conformity with the present Covenant, the State may subject such rights only to such limitations as are determined by law only in so far as this may be compatible with the nature of these rights and solely for the purpose of promoting the general welfare in a democratic society.

Article 5

1.   Nothing in the present Covenant may be interpreted as implying for any State, group or person any right to engage in any activity or to perform any act aimed at the destruction of any of the rights or freedoms recognized herein, or at their limitation to a greater extent than is provided for in the present Covenant.

2. No restriction upon or derogation from any of the fundamental human rights recognized or existing in any country in virtue of law, conventions, regulations or custom shall be admitted on the pretext that the present Covenant does not recognize such rights or that it recognizes them to a lesser extent.

PART III

Article 6

1. The States Parties to the present Covenant recognize the right to work, which includes the right of everyone to the opportunity to gain his living by work which he freely chooses or accepts, and will take appropriate steps to safeguard this right.

2. The steps to be taken by a State Party to the present Covenant to achieve the full realization of this right shall include technical and vocational guidance and training programmes, policies and techniques to achieve steady economic, social and cultural development and full and productive employment under conditions safeguarding fundamental political and economic freedoms to the individual.

Article 7

The States Parties to the present Covenant recognize the right of everyone to the enjoyment of just and favourable conditions of work which ensure, in particular:

(a) Remuneration which provides all workers, as a minimum, with:

(i) Fair wages and equal remuneration for work of equal value without distinction of any kind, in particular women being guaranteed conditions of work not inferior to those enjoyed by men, with equal pay for equal work;

(ii) A decent living for themselves and their families in accordance with the provisions of the present Covenant;

(b) Safe and healthy working conditions;

(c) Equal opportunity for everyone to be promoted in his employment to an appropriate higher level, subject to no considerations other than those of seniority and competence;

(d) Rest, leisure and reasonable limitation of working hours and periodic holidays with pay, as well as remuneration for public holidays.

Article 8

1. The States Parties to the present Covenant undertake to ensure:

(*a*) The right of everyone to form trade unions and join the trade union of his choice, subject only to the rules of the organization concerned, for the promotion and protection of his economic and social interests. No restrictions may be placed on the exercise of this right other than those prescribed by law and which are necessary in a democratic society in the interests of national security or public order or for the protection of the rights and freedoms of others;

(*b*) The right of trade unions to establish national federations or confederations and the right of the latter to form or join international trade-union organizations;

(*c*) The right of trade unions to function freely subject to no limitations other than those prescribed by law and which are necessary in a democratic society in the interests of national security or public order or for the protection of the rights and freedoms of others;

(*d*) The right to strike, provided that it is exercised in conformity with the laws of the particular country.

2. This article shall not prevent the imposition of lawful restrictions on the exercise of these rights by members of the armed forces or of the police or of the administration of the State.

3. Nothing in this article shall authorize States Parties to the International Labour Organisation Convention of 1948 concerning Freedom of Association and Protection of the Right to Organize to take legislative measures which would prejudice, or apply the law in such a manner as would prejudice, the guarantees provided for in that Convention.

Article 9

The States Parties to the present Covenant recognize the right of everyone to social security, including social insurance.

Article 10

The States Parties to the present Covenant recognize that:

1. The widest possible protection and assistance should be accorded to the family, which is the natural and fundamental group unit of society, particularly for its establishment and while it is responsible for the care and education of dependent children. Marriage must be entered into with the free consent of the intending spouses.

2. Special protection should be accorded to mothers during a reasonable period before and after childbirth. During such period working mothers should be accorded paid leave or leave with adequate social security benefits.

3. Special measures of protection and assistance should be taken on behalf of all children and young persons without any discrimination for

reasons of parentage or other conditions. Children and young persons should be protected from economic and social exploitation. Their employment in work harmful to their morals or health or dangerous to life or likely to hamper their normal development should be punishable by law. States should also set age limits below which the paid employment of child labour should be prohibited and punishable by law.

Article 11

1.   The States Parties to the present Covenant recognize the right of everyone to an adequate standard of living for himself and his family, including adequate food, clothing and housing, and to the continuous improvement of living conditions. The States Parties will take appropriate steps to ensure the realization of this right, recognizing to this effect the essential importance of international co-operation based on free consent.

2.   The States Parties to the present Covenant, recognizing the fundamental right of everyone to be free from hunger, shall take, individually and through international co-operation, the measures, including specific programmes, which are needed:

(a) To improve methods of production, conservation and distribution of food by making full use of technical and scientific knowledge, by disseminating knowledge of the principles of nutrition and by developing or reforming agrarian systems in such a way as to achieve the most efficient development and utilization of natural resources;

(b) Taking into account the problems of both food-importing and food-exporting countries, to ensure an equitable distribution of world food supplies in relation to need.

Article 12

1.   The States Parties to the present Covenant recognize the right of everyone to the enjoyment of the highest attainable standard of physical and mental health.

2.   The steps to be taken by the States Parties to the present Covenant to achieve the full realization of this right shall include those necessary for:

(a) The provision for the reduction of the stillbirth-rate and of infant mortality and for the healthy development of the child;

(b) The improvement of all aspects of environmental and industrial hygiene;

(c) The prevention, treatment and control of epidemic, endemic, occupational and other diseases;

(d) The creation of conditions which would assure to all medical service and medical attention in the event of sickness.

Article 13

1. The States Parties to the present Covenant recognize the right of everyone to education. They agree that education shall be directed to the full development of the human personality and the sense of its dignity, and shall strengthen the respect for human rights and fundamental freedoms. They further agree that education shall enable all persons to participate effectively in a free society, promote understanding, tolerance and friendship among all nations and all racial, ethnic or religious groups, and further the activities of the United Nations for the maintenance of peace.

2. The States Parties to the present Covenant recognize that, with a view to achieving the full realization of this right:

(a) Primary education shall be compulsory and available free to all;

(b) Secondary education in its different forms, including technical and vocational secondary education, shall be made generally available and accessible to all by every appropriate means, and in particular by the progressive introduction of free education;

(c) Higher education shall be made equally accessible to all, on the basis of capacity, by every appropriate means, and in particular by the progressive introduction of free education;

(d) Fundamental education shall be encouraged or intensified as far as possible for those persons who have not received or completed the whole period of their primary education;

(e) The development of a system of schools at all levels shall be actively pursued, an adequate fellowship system shall be established, and the material conditions of teaching staff shall be continuously improved.

3. The States Parties to the present Covenant undertake to have respect for the liberty of parents and, when applicable, legal guardians to choose for their children schools, other than those established by the public authorities, which conform to such minimum educational standards as may be laid down or approved by the State and to ensure the religious and moral education of their children in conformity with their own convictions.

4. No part of this article shall be construed so as to interfere with the liberty of individuals and bodies to establish and direct educational institutions, subject always to the observance of the principles set forth in paragraph 1 of this article and to the requirement that the education given in such institutions shall conform to such minimum standards as may be laid down by the State.

Article 14

Each State Party to the present Covenant which, at the time of becoming a Party, has not been able to secure in its metropolitan territory or other territories under its jurisdiction compulsory primary education, free of charge, undertakes, within two years, to work out and adopt a detailed plan of action for the progressive implementation, within a reasonable number of years, to be fixed in the plan, of the principle of compulsory education free of charge for all.

Article 15

1.   The States Parties to the present Covenant recognize the right of everyone:

(a) To take part in cultural life;

(b) To enjoy the benefits of scientific progress and its applications;

(c) To benefit from the protection of the moral and material interests resulting from any scientific, literary or artistic production of which he is the author.

2.   The steps to be taken by the States Parties to the present Covenant to achieve the full realization of this right shall include those necessary for the conservation, the development and the diffusion of science and culture.

3.   The States Parties to the present Covenant undertake to respect the freedom indispensable for scientific research and creative activity.

4.   The States Parties to the present Covenant recognize the benefits to be derived from the encouragement and development of international contacts and co-operation in the scientific and cultural fields.

PART IV

Article 16

1.   The States Parties to the present Covenant undertake to submit in conformity with this part of the Covenant reports on the measures which they have adopted and the progress made in achieving the observance of the rights recognized herein.

2.   (a) All reports shall be submitted to the Secretary-General of the United Nations, who shall transmit copies to the Economic and Social Council for consideration in accordance with the provisions of the present Covenant;

(b) The Secretary-General of the United Nations shall also transmit to the specialized agencies copies of the reports, or any relevant parts therefrom, from States Parties to the present Covenant which are also members of these specialized agencies in so far as these reports, or parts therefrom, relate to any matters which fall within the responsibilities of the said agencies in accordance with their constitutional instruments.

Article 17

1.   The States Parties to the present Covenant shall furnish their reports in stages, in accordance with a programme to be established by the Economic

and Social Council within one year of the entry into force of the present Covenant after consultation with the States Parties and the specialized agencies concerned.

2.   Reports may indicate factors and difficulties affecting the degree of fulfilment of obligations under the present Covenant.

3.   Where relevant information has previously been furnished to the United Nations or to any specialized agency by any State Party to the present Covenant, it will not be necessary to reproduce that information, but a precise reference to the information so furnished will suffice.

Article 18

Pursuant to its responsibilities under the Charter of the United Nations in the field of human rights and fundamental freedoms, the Economic and Social Council may make arrangements with the specialized agencies in respect of their reporting to it on the progress made in achieving the observance of the provisions of the present Covenant falling within the scope of their activities. These reports may include particulars of decisions and recommendations on such implementation adopted by their competent organs.

Article 19

The Economic and Social Council may transmit to the Commission on Human Rights for study and general recommendation or, as appropriate, for information the reports concerning human rights submitted by States in accordance with articles 16 and 17, and those concerning human rights submitted by the specialized agencies in accordance with article 18.

Article 20

The States Parties to the present Covenant and the specialized agencies concerned may submit comments to the Economic and Social Council on any general recommendation under article 19 or reference to such general recommendation in any report of the Commission on Human Rights or any documentation referred to therein.

Article 21

The Economic and Social Council may submit from time to time to the General Assembly reports with recommendations of a general nature and a summary of the information received from the States Parties to the present Covenant and the specialized agencies on the measures taken and the progress made in achieving general observance of the rights recognized in the present Covenant.

Article 22

The Economic and Social Council may bring to the attention of other organs of the United Nations, their subsidiary organs and specialized agencies concerned with furnishing technical assistance any matters arising out of the reports referred to in this part of the present Covenant which may assist such bodies in deciding, each within its field of competence, on the advisability of international measures likely to contribute to the effective progressive implementation of the present Covenant.

Article 23

The States Parties to the present Covenant agree that international action for the achievement of the rights recognized in the present Covenant includes such methods as the conclusion of conventions, the adoption of recommendations, the furnishing of technical assistance and the holding of regional meetings and technical meetings for the purpose of consultation and study organized in conjunction with the Governments concerned.

Article 24

Nothing in the present Covenant shall be interpreted as impairing the provisions of the Charter of the United Nations and of the constitutions of the specialized agencies which define the respective responsibilities of the various organs of the United Nations and of the specialized agencies in regard to the matters dealt with in the present Covenant.

Article 25

Nothing in the present Covenant shall be interpreted as impairing the inherent right of all peoples to enjoy and utilize fully and freely their natural wealth and resources.

Part V

Article 26

1. The present Covenant is open for signature by any State Member of the United Nations or member of any of its specialized agencies, by any State Party to the Statute of the International Court of Justice, and by any other State which has been invited by the General Assembly of the United Nations to become a party to the present Covenant.

2. The present Covenant is subject to ratification. Instruments of ratification shall be deposited with the Secretary-General of the United Nations.

3. The present Covenant shall be open to accession by any State referred to in paragraph 1 of this article.

4. Accession shall be effected by the deposit of an instrument of accession with the Secretary-General of the United Nations.

5. The Secretary-General of the United Nations shall inform all States which have signed the present Covenant or acceded to it of the deposit of each instrument of ratification or accession.

Article 27

1. The present Covenant shall enter into force three months after the date of the deposit with the Secretary-General of the United Nations of the thirty-fifth instrument of ratification or instrument of accession.

2. For each State ratifying the present Covenant or acceding to it after the deposit of the thirty-fifth instrument of ratification or instrument of accession, the present Covenant shall enter into force three months after the date of the deposit of its own instrument of ratification or instrument of accession.

Article 28

The provisions of the present Covenant shall extend to all parts of federal States wihout any limitations or exceptions.

Article 29

1. Any State Party to the present Covenant may propose an amendment and file it with the Secretary-General of the United Nations. The Secretary-General shall thereupon communicate any proposed amendments to the States Parties to the present Covenant with a request that they notify him whether they favour a conference of States Parties for the purpose of considering and voting upon the proposals. In the event that at least one third of the States Parties favours such a conference, the Secretary-General shall convene the conference under the auspices of the United Nations. Any amendment adopted by a majority of the States Parties present and voting at the conference shall be submitted to the General Assembly of the United Nations for approval.

2. Amendments shall come into force when they have been approved by the General Assembly of the United Nations and accepted by a two-thirds majority of the States Parties to the present Covenant in accordance with their respective constitutional processes.

3. When amendments come into force they shall be binding on those States Parties which have accepted them, other States Parties still being bound by the provisions of the present Covenant and any earlier amendment which they have accepted.

Article 30

Irrespective of the notifications made under article 26, paragraph 5, the Secretary-General of the United Nations shall inform all States referred to in paragraph 1 of the same article of the following particulars:

(*a*) Signatures, ratifications and accessions under article 26;

(*b*) The date of the entry into force of the present Covenant under article 27 and the date of the entry into force of any amendments under article 29.

Article 31

1.   The present Covenant, of which the Chinese, English, French, Russian and Spanish texts are equally authentic, shall be deposited in the archives of the United Nations.

2.   The Secretary-General of the United Nations shall transmit certified copies of the present Covenant to all States referred to in article 26.

International Covenant on Civil and Political Rights

Adopted and opened for signature, ratification and accession by General Assembly resolution 2200 A (XXI) of 16 December 1966

ENTRY INTO FORCE: 23 March 1976, in accordance with article 49

PREAMBLE

The States Parties to the present Covenant,

Considering that, in accordance with the principles proclaimed in the Charter of the United Nations, recognition of the inherent dignity and of the equal and inalienable rights of all members of the human family is the foundation of freedom, justice and peace in the world,

Recognizing that these rights derive from the inherent dignity of the human person,

Recognizing that, in accordance with the Universal Declaration of Human rights, the ideal of free human beings enjoying civil and political freedom and freedom from fear and want can only be achieved if conditions are created whereby everyone may enjoy his civil and political rights, as well as his economic, social and cultural rights,

Considering the obligation of States under the Charter of the United Nations to promote universal respect for, and observance of, human rights and freedoms,

Realizing that the individual, having duties to other individuals and to the community to which he belongs, is under a responsibility to strive for the promotion and observance of the rights recognized in the present Covenant,

Agree upon the following articles:

Part I

Article 1

1. All peoples have the right of self-determination. By virtue of that right they freely determine their political status and freely pursue their economic, social and cultural development.

2. All peoples may, for their own ends, freely dispose of their natural wealth and resources without prejudice to any obligations arising out of international economic co-operation, based upon the principle of mutual benefit, and international law. In no case may a people be deprived of its own means of subsistence.

3. The States Parties to the present Covenant, including those having responsibility for the administration of Non-Self-Governing and Trust Territories, shall promote the realization of the right of self-determination, and shall respect that right, in conformity with the provisions of the Charter of the United Nations.

Part II

Article 2

1. Each State Party to the present Covenant undertakes to respect and to ensure to all individuals within its territory and subject to its jurisdiction the rights recognized in the present Covenant, without distinction of any kind, such as race, colour, sex, language, religion, political or other opinion, national or social origin, property, birth or other status.

2. Where not already provided for by existing legislative or other measures, each State Party to the present Covenant undertakes to take the necessary steps, in accordance with its constitutional processes and with the provisions of the present Covenant, to adopt such legislative or other measures as may be necessary to give effect to the rights recognized in the present Covenant.

3. Each State Party to the present Covenant undertakes:

(a) To ensure that any person whose rights or freedoms as herein recognized are violated shall have an effective remedy, notwithstanding that the violation has been committed by persons acting in an official capacity;

(b) To ensure that any person claiming such a remedy shall have his right thereto determined by competent judicial, administrative or legislative authorities, or by any other competent authority provided for by the legal system of the State, and to develop the possibilities of judicial remedy;

(c) To ensure that the competent authorities shall enforce such remedies when granted.

Article 3

The States Parties to the present Covenant undertake to ensure the equal right of men and women to the enjoyment of all civil and political rights set forth in the present Covenant.

Article 4

1. In time of public emergency which threatens the life of the nation and the existence of which is officially proclaimed, the States Parties to the present Covenant may take measures derogating from their obligations under the present Covenant to the extent strictly required by the exigencies of the situation, provided that such measures are not inconsistent with their other obligations under international law and do not involve discrimination solely on the ground of race, colour, sex, language, religion or social origin.

2. No derogation from articles 6, 7, 8 (paragraphs 1 and 2), 11, 15, 16 and 18 may be made under this provision.

3. Any State Party to the present Covenant availing itself of the right of derogation shall immediately inform the other States Parties to the present Covenant, through the intermediary of the Secretary-General of the United Nations, of the provisions from which it has derogated and of the reasons by which it was actuated. A further communication shall be made, through the same intermediary, on the date on which it terminates such derogation.

Article 5

1. Nothing in the present Covenant may be interpreted as implying for any State, group or person any right to engage in any activity or perform any act aimed at the destruction of any of the rights and freedoms recognized herein or at their limitation to a greater extent than is provided for in the present Covenant.

2. There shall be no restriction upon or derogation from any of the fundamental human rights recognized or existing in any State Party to the present Covenant pursuant to law, conventions, regulations or custom on the pretext that the present Covenant does not recognize such rights or that it recognizes them to a lesser extent.

PART III

Article 6

1. Every human being has the inherent right to life. This right shall be protected by law. No one shall be arbitrarily deprived of his life.

2. In countries which have not abolished the death penalty, sentence of death may be imposed only for the most serious crimes in accordance with the law in force at the time of the commission of the crime and not contrary to the provisions of the present Covenant and to the Convention on the Prevention

and Punishment of the Crime of Genocide. This penalty can only be carried out pursuant to a final judgement rendered by a competent court.

3. When deprivation of life constitutes the crime of genocide, it is understood that nothing in this article shall authorize any State Party to the present Covenant to derogate in any way from any obligation assumed under the provisions of the Convention on the Prevention and Punishment of the Crime of Genocide.

4. Anyone sentenced to death shall have the right to seek pardon or commutation of the sentence. Amnesty, pardon or commutation of the sentence of death may be granted in all cases.

5. Sentence of death shall not be imposed for crimes committed by persons below eighteen years of age and shall not be carried out on pregnant women.

6. Nothing in this article shall be invoked to delay or to prevent the abolition of capital punishement by any State Party to the present Covenant.

Article 7

No one shall be subjected to torture or to cruel, inhuman or degrading treatment or punishment. In particular, no one shall be subjected without his free consent to medical or scientific experimentation.

Article 8

1. No one shall be held in slavery; slavery and the slave-trade in all their forms shall be prohibited.

2. No one shall be held in servitude.

3. (a) No one shall be required to perform forced or compulsory labour;

(b) Paragraph 3 (a) shall not be held to preclude, in countries where imprisonment with hard labour may be imposed as a punishment for a crime, the performance of hard labour in pursuance of a sentence to such punishment by a competent court;

(c) For the purpose of this paragraph the term "forced or compulsory labour" shall not include:

(i) Any work or service, not referred to in subparagraph (b), normally required of a person who is under detention in consequence of a lawful order of a court, or of a person during conditional release from such detention;

(ii) Any service of a military character and, in countries where conscientious objection is recognized, any national service required by law of conscientious objectors;

(iii) Any service exacted in cases of emergency or calamity threatening the life or well-being of the community;

(iv) Any work or service which forms part of normal civil obligations.

Article 9

1. Everyone has the right to liberty and security of person. No one shall be subjected to arbitrary arrest or detention. No one shall be deprived of his liberty except on such grounds and in accordance with such procedure as are established by law.

2. Anyone who is arrested shall be informed, at the time of arrest, of the reasons for his arrest and shall be promptly informed of any charges against him.

3. Anyone arrested or detained on a criminal charge shall be brought promptly before a judge or other officer authorized by law to exercise judicial power and shall be entitled to trial within a reasonable time or to release. It shall not be the general rule that persons awaiting trial shall be detained in custody, but release may be subject to guarantees to appear for trial, at any other stage of the judicial proceedings, and, should occasion arise, for execution of the judgement.

4. Anyone who is deprived of his liberty by arrest or detention shall be entitled to take proceedings before a court, in order that that court may decide without delay on the lawfulness of his detention and order his release if the detention is not lawful.

5. Anyone who has been victim of unlawful arrest or detention shall have an enforceable right to compensation.

Article 10

1. All persons deprived of their liberty shall be treated with humanity and with respect for the inherent dignity of the human person.

2. (a) Accused persons shall, save in exceptional circumstances, be segregated from convicted persons and shall be subject to separate treatment appropriate to their status as unconvicted persons;

(b) Accused juvenile persons shall be separated from adults and brought as speedily as possible for adjudication.

3. The penitentiary system shall comprise treatment of prisoners the essential aim of which shall be their reformation and social rehabilitation. Juvenile offenders shall be segregated from adults and be accorded treatment appropriate to their age and legal status.

Article 11

No one shall be imprisoned merely on the ground of inability to fulfil a contractual obligation.

Article 12

1. Everyone lawfully within the territory of a State shall, within that territory, have the right to liberty of movement and freedom to choose his residence.

2. Everyone shall be free to leave any country, including his own.

3. The above-mentioned rights shall not be subject to any restrictions except those which are provided by law, are necessary to protect national security, public order (*ordre public*), public health or morals or the rights and freedoms of others, and are consistent with the other rights recognized in the present Covenant.

4. No one shall be arbitrarily deprived of the right to enter his own country.

Article 13

An alien lawfully in the territory of a State Party to the present Covenant may be expelled therefrom only in pursuance of a decision reached in accordance with law and shall, except where compelling reasons of national security otherwise require, be allowed to submit the reasons against his expulsion and to have his case reviewed by, and be represented for the purpose before, the competent authority or a person or persons especially designated by the competent authority.

Article 14

1. All persons shall be equal before the courts and tribunals. In the determination of any criminal charge against him, or of his rights and obligations in a suit at law, everyone shall be entitled to a fair and public hearing by a competent, independent and impartial tribunal established by law. The press and the public may be excluded from all or part of a trial for reasons of morals, public order (*ordre public*) or national security in a democratic society, or when the interest of the private lives of the Parties so requires, or to the extent strictly necessary in the opinion of the court in special circumstances where publicity would prejudice the interests of justice; but any judgement rendered in a criminal case or in a suit at law shall be made public except where the interest of juvenile persons otherwise requires or the proceedings concern matrimonial disputes of the guardianship of children.

2. Everyone charged with a criminal offence shall have the right to be presumed innocent until proved guilty according to law.

3. In the determination of any criminal charge against him, everyone shall be entitled to the following minimum guarantees, in full equality:

(*a*) To be informed promptly and in detail in a language which he understands of the nature and cause of the charge against him;

(*b*) To have adequate time and facilities for the preparation of his defence and to communicate with counsel of his own choosing;

(c) To be tried without undue delay;

(d) To be tried in his presence, and to defend himself in person or through legal assistance of his own choosing; to be informed, if he does not have legal assistance, of this right; and to have legal assistance assigned to him, in any case where the interests of justice so require, and without payment by him in any such case if he does not have sufficient means to pay for it;

(e) To examine, or have examined, the witnesses against him and to obtain the attendance and examination of witnesses on his behalf under the same conditions as witnesses against him;

(f) To have the free assistance of an interpreter if he cannot understand or speak the language used in court;

(g) Not to be compelled to testify against himself or to confess guilt.

4. In the case of juvenile persons, the procedure shall be such as will take account of their age and the desirability of promoting their re-habilitation.

5. Everyone convicted of a crime shall have the right to his conviction and sentence being reviewed by a higher tribunal according to law.

6. When a person has by a final decision been convicted of a criminal offence and when subsequently his conviction has been reversed or he has been pardoned on the ground that a new or newly discovered fact shows conclusively that there has been a miscarriage of justice, the person who has suffered punishment as a result of such conviction shall be compensated according to law, unless it is proved that the non-disclosure of the unknown fact in time is wholly or partly attributable to him.

7. No one shall be liable to be tried or punished again for an offence for which he has already been finally convicted or acquitted in accordance with the law and penal procedure of each country.

Article 15

1. No one shall be held guilty of any criminal offence on account of any act or omission which did not constitute a criminal offence, under national or international law, at the time when it was committed. Nor shall a heavier penalty be imposed than the one that was applicable at the time when the criminal offence was committed. If, subsequent to the commission of the offence, provision is made by law for the imposition of the lighter penalty, the offender shall benefit thereby.

2. Nothing in this article shall prejudice the trial and punishment of any person for any act or omission which, at the time when it was committed, was criminal according to the general principles of law recognized by the community of nations.

Article 16

Everyone shall have the right to recognition everywhere as a person before the law.

Article 17

1.   No one shall be subjected to arbitrary or unlawful interference with his privacy, family, home or correspondence, nor to unlawful attacks on his honour and reputation.

2.   Everyone has the right to the protection of the law against such interference or attacks.

Article 18

1.   Everyone shall have the right to freedom of thought, conscience and religion. This right shall include freedom to have or to adopt a religion or belief of his choice, and freedom, either individually or in community with others and in public or private, to manifest his religion or belief in worship, observance, practice and teaching.

2.   No one shall be subject to coercion which would impair his freedom to have or to adopt a religion or belief of his choice.

3.   Freedom to manifest one's religion or beliefs may be subject only to such limitations as are prescribed by law and are necessary to protect public safety, order, health, or morals or the fundamental rights and freedoms of others.

4.   The States Parties to the present Covenant undertake to have respect for the liberty of parents and, when applicable, legal guardians to ensure the religious and moral education of their children in conformity with their own convictions.

Article 19

1.   Everyone shall have the right to hold opinions without interference.

2.   Everyone shall have the right to freedom of expression; this right shall include freedom to seek, receive and impart information and ideas of all kinds, regardless of frontiers, either orally, in writing or in print, in the form of art, or through any other media of his choice.

3.   The exercise of the rights provided for in paragraph 2 of this article carries with it special duties and responsibilities. It may therefore be subject to certain restrictions, but these shall only be such as are provided by law and are necessary:

(a) For respect of the rights or reputations of others;

(b) For the protection of national security or of public order (ordre public), or of public health or morals.

Article 20

1.   Any propaganda for war shall be prohibited by law.

2.   Any advocacy of national, racial or religious hatred that constitutes incitement to discrimination, hostility or violence shall be prohibited by law.

Article 21

The right of peaceful assembly shall be recognized. No restrictions may be placed on the exercise of this right other than those imposed in conformity with the law and which are necessary in a democratic society in the interests of national security or public safety, public order (*ordre public*), the protection of public health or morals or the protection of the rights and freedoms of others.

Article 22

1.   Everyone shall have the right to freedom of association with others, including the right to form and join trade unions for the protection of his interests.

2.   No restrictions may be placed on the exercise of this right other than those which are prescribed by law and which are necessary in a democratic society in the interests of national security or public safety, public order (*ordre public*), the protection of public health or morals or the protection of the rights and freedoms of others. This article shall not prevent the imposition of lawful restrictions on members of the armed forces and of the police in their exercise of this right.

3.   Nothing in this article shall authorize States Parties to the International Labour Organisation Convention of 1948 concerning Freedom of Association and Protection of the Right to Organize to take legislative measures which would prejudice, or to apply the law in such a manner as to prejudice the guarantees provided for in that Convention.

Article 23

1.   The family is the natural and fundamental group unit of society and is entitled to protection by society and the State.

2.   The right of men and women of marriageable age to marry and to found a family shall be recognized.

3.   No marriage shall be entered into without the free and full consent of the intending spouses.

4.   States Parties to the present Covenant shall take appropriate steps to ensure equality of rights and responsibilities of spouses as to marriage, during marriage and at its dissolution. In the case of dissolution, provision shall be made for the necessary protection of any children.

Article 24

1. Every child shall have, without any discrimination as to race, colour, sex, language, religion, national or social origin, property or birth, the right to such measures of protection as are required by his status as a minor, on the part of his family, society and the State.

2. Every child shall be registered immediately after birth and shall have a name.

3. Every child has the right to acquire a nationality.

Article 25

Every citizen shall have the right and the opportunity, without any of the distinctions mentioned in article 2 and without unreasonable restrictions:

(a) To take part in the conduct of public affairs, directly or through freely chosen representatives;

(b) To vote and to be elected at genuine periodic elections which shall be by universal and equal suffrage and shall be held by secret ballot, guaranteeing the free expression of the will of the electors;

(c) To have access, on general terms of equality, to public service in his country.

Article 26

All persons are equal before the law and are entitled without any discrimination to the equal protection of the law. In this respect, the law shall prohibit any discrimination and guarantee to all persons equal and effective protection against discrimination on any ground such as race, colour, sex, language, religion, political or other opinion, national or social origin, property, birth or other status.

Article 27

In those States in which ethnic, religious or linguistic minorities exist, persons belonging to such minorities shall not be denied the right, in community with the other members of their group, to enjoy their own culture, to profess and practise their own religion, or to use their own language.

PART IV

Article 28

1. There shall be established a Human Rights Committee (hereafter referred to in the present Covenant as the Committee). It shall consist of eighteen members and shall carry out the functions hereinafter provided.

2. The Committee shall be composed of nationals of the States Parties to the present Covenant who shall be persons of high moral character and recognized competence in the field of human rights, consideration being given to the usefulness of the participation of some persons having legal experience.

3. The members of the Committee shall be elected and shall serve in their personal capacity.

Article 29

1. The members of the Committee shall be elected by secret ballot from a list of persons possessing the qualifications prescribed in article 28 and nominated for the purpose by the States Parties to the present Covenant.

2. Each State Party to the present Covenant may nominate not more than two persons. These persons shall be nationals of the nominating State.

3. A person shall be eligible for renomination.

Article 30

1. The initial election shall be held no later than six months after the date of the entry into force of the present Covenant.

2. At least four months before the date of each election to the Committee, other than an election to fill a vacancy declared in accordance with article 34, the Secretary-General of the United Nations shall address a written invitation to the States Parties to the present Covenant to submit their nominations for membership of the Committee within three months.

3. The Secretary-General of the United Nations shall prepare a list in alphabetical order of all the persons thus nominated, with an indication of the States Parties which have nominated them, and shall submit it to the States Parties to the present Covenant no later than one month before the date of each election.

4. Elections of the members of the Committee shall be held at a meeting of the States Parties to the present Covenant convened by the Secretary-General of the United Nations at the Headquarters of the United Nations. At that meeting, for which two thirds of the States Parties to the present Covenant shall constitute a quorum, the persons elected to the Committee shall be those nominees who obtain the largest number of votes and an absolute majority of the votes of the representatives of States Parties present and voting.

Article 31

1. The Committee may not include more than one national of the same State.

2.   In the election of the Committee, consideration shall be given to equitable geographical distribution of membership and to the representation of the different forms of civilization and of the principal legal systems.

Article 32

1.   The members of the Committee shall be elected for a term of four years. They shall be eligible for re-election if renominated. However, the terms of nine of the members elected at the first election shall expire at the end of two years; immediately after the first election, the names of these nine members shall be chosen by lot by the Chairman of the meeting referred to in article 30, paragraph 4.

2.   Elections at the expiry of office shall be held in accordance with the preceding articles of this part of the present Covenant.

Article 33

1.   If, in the unanimous opinion of the other members, a member of the Committee has ceased to carry out his functions for any cause other than absence of a temporary character, the Chairman of the Committee shall notify the Secretary-General of the United Nations, who shall then declare the seat of that member to be vacant.

2.   In the event of the death or the resignation of a member of the Committee, the Chairman shall immediately notify the Secretary-General of the United Nations, who shall declare the seat vacant from the date of death or the date on which the resignation takes effect.

Article 34

1.   When a vacancy is declared in accordance with article 33 and if the term of office of the member to be replaced does not expire within six months of the declaration of the vacancy, the Secretary-General of the United Nations shall notify each of the States Parties to the present Covenant, which may within two months submit nominations in accordance with article 29 for the purpose of filling the vacancy.

2.   The Secretary-General of the United Nations shall prepare a list in alphabetical order of the persons thus nominated and shall submit it to the States Parties to the present Covenant. The election to fill the vacancy shall then take place in accordance with the relevant provisions of this part of the present Covenant.

3.   A member of the Committee elected to fill a vacancy declared in accordance with article 33 shall hold office for the remainder of the term of the member who vacated the seat on the Committee under the provisions of that article.

Article 35

The members of the Committee shall, with the approval of the General Assembly of the United Nations, receive emoluments from United Nations resources on such terms and conditions as the General Assembly may decide, having regard to the importance of the Committee's responsibilities.

Article 36

The Secretary-General of the United Nations shall provide the necessary staff and facilities for the effective performance of the functions of the Committee under the present Covenant.

Article 37

1. The Secretary-General of the United Nations shall convene the initial meeting of the Committee at the Headquarters of the United Nations.

2. After its initial meeting, the Committee shall meet at such times as shall be provided in its rules of procedure.

3. The Committee shall normally meet at the Headquarters of the United Nations or at the United Nations Office at Geneva.

Article 38

Every member of the Committee shall, before taking up his duties, make a solemn declaration in open committee that he will perform his functions impartially and conscientiously.

Article 39

1. The Committee shall elect its officers for a term of two years. They may be re-elected.

2. The Committee shall establish its own rules of procedure, but these rules shall provide, *inter alia*, that:

(a) Twelve members shall constitute a quorum;

(b) Decisions of the Committee shall be made by a majority vote of the members present.

Article 40

1. The States Parties to the present Covenant undertake to submit reports on the measures they have adopted which give effect to the rights recognized herein and on the progress made in the enjoyment of those rights:

(a) Within one year of the entry into force of the present Covenant for the States Parties concerned;

(b) Thereafter whenever the Committee so requests.

2.   All reports shall be submitted to the Secretary-General of the United Nations, who shall transmit them to the Committee for consideration. Reports shall indicate the factors and difficulties, if any, affecting the implementation of the present Covenant.

3.   The Secretary-General of the United Nations may, after consultation with the Committee, transmit to the specialized agencies concerned copies of such parts of the reports as may fall within their field of competence.

4.   The Committee shall study the reports submitted by the States Parties to the present Covenant. It shall transmit its reports, and such general comments as it may consider appropriate, to the States Parties. The Committee may also transmit to the Economic and Social Council these comments along with the copies of the reports it has received from States Parties to the present Covenant.

5.   The States Parties to the present Covenant may submit to the Committee observations on any comments that may be made in accordance with paragraph 4 of this article.

Article 41

1.   A State Party to the present Covenant may at any time declare under this article that it recognizes the competence of the Committee to receive and consider communications to the effect that a State Party claims that another State Party is not fulfilling its obligations under the present Covenant. Communications under this article may be received and considered only if submitted by a State Party which has made a declaration recognizing in regard to itself the competence of the Committee. No communication shall be received by the Committee if it concerns a State Party which has not made such a declaration. Communications received under this article shall be dealt with in accordance with the following procedure:

(*a*) If a State Party to the present Covenant considers that another State Party is not giving effect to the provisions of the present Covenant, it may, by written communication, bring the matter to the attention of that State Party. Within three months after the receipt of the communication the receiving State shall afford the State which sent the communication an explanation, or any other statement in writing clarifying the matter which should include, to the extent possible and pertinent, reference to domestic procedures and remedies taken, pending, or available in the matter;

(*b*) If the matter is not adjusted to the satisfaction of both States Parties concerned within six months after the receipt by the receiving State of the initial communication, either State shall have the right to refer the matter to the Committee, by notice given to the Committee and to the other State;

(*c*) The Committee shall deal with a matter referred to it only after it has ascertained that all available domestic remedies have been invoked and exhausted in the matter, in conformity with the generally recognized principles of international law. This shall not be the rule where the application of the remedies is unreasonably prolonged;

(d) The Committee shall hold closed meetings when examining communications under this article;

(e) Subject to the provisions of subparagraph (c), the Committee shall make available its good offices to the States Parties concerned with a view to a friendly solution of the matter on the basis of respect for human rights and fundamental freedoms as recognized in the present Covenant;

(f) In any matter referred to it, the Committee may call upon the States Parties concerned, referred to in subparagraph (b), to supply any relevant information;

(g) The States Parties concerned, referred to in subparagraph (b), shall have the right to be represented when the matter is being considered in the Committee and to make submissions orally and/or in writing;

(h) The Committee shall, within twelve months after the date of receipt of notice under subparagraph (b), submit a report:

(i) If a solution within the terms of subparagraph (e) is reached, the Committee shall confine its report to a brief statement of the facts and of the solution reached;

(ii) If a solution within the terms of subparagraph (e) is not reached, the Committee shall confine its report to a brief statement of the facts; the written submissions and record of the oral submissions made by the States Parties concerned shall be attached to the report.

In every matter, the report shall be communicated to the States Parties concerned.

2. The provisions of this article shall come into force when ten States Parties to the present Covenant have made declarations under paragraph 1 of this article. Such declarations shall be deposited by the States Parties with the Secretary-General of the United Nations, who shall transmit copies thereof to the other States Parties. A declaration may be withdrawn at any time by notification to the Secretary-General. Such a withdrawal shall not prejudice the consideration of any matter which is the subject of a communication already transmitted under this article; no further communication by any State Party shall be received after the notification of withdrawal of the declaration has been received by the Secretary-General, unless the State Party concerned has made a new declaration.

Article 42

1. (a) If a matter referred to the Committee in accordance with article 41 is not resolved to the satisfaction of the States Parties concerned, the Committee may, with the prior consent of the States Parties concerned, appoint an *ad hoc* Conciliation Commission (hereinafter referred to as the

Commission). The good offices of the Commission shall be made available to the States Parties concerned with a view to an amicable solution of the matter on the basis of respect for the present Covenant;

(b) The Commission shall consist of five persons acceptable to the States Parties concerned. If the States Parties concerned fail to reach agreement within three months on all or part of the composition of the Commission, the members of the Commission concerning whom no agreement has been reached shall be elected by secret ballot by a two-thirds majority vote of the Committee from among its members.

2. The members of the Commission shall serve in their personal capacity. They shall not be nationals of the States Parties concerned, or of a State not Party to the present Covenant, or of a State Party which has not made a declaration under article 41.

3. The Commission shall elect its own Chairman and adopt its own rules of procedure.

4. The meetings of the Commission shall normally be held at the Headquarters of the United Nations or at the United Nations Office at Geneva. However, they may be held at such other convenient places as the Commission may determine in consultation with the Secretary-General of the United Nations and the States Parties concerned.

5. The secretariat provided in acordance with article 36 shall also service the commissions appointed under this article.

6. The information received and collated by the Committee shall be made available to the Commission and the Commission may call upon the States Parties concerned to supply any other relevant information.

7. When the Commission has fully considered the matter, but in any event not later than twelve months after having been seized of the matter, it shall submit to the Chairman of the Committee a report for communication to the States Parties concerned:

(a) If the Commission is unable to complete its consideration of the matter within twelve months, it shall confine its report to a brief statement of the status of its consideration of the matter;

(b) If an amicable solution to the matter on the basis of respect for human rights as recognized in the present Covenant is reached, the Commission shall confine its report to a brief statement of the facts and of the solution reached;

(c) If a solution within the terms of subparagraph (b) is not reached, the Commission's report shall embody its findings on all questions of fact relevant to the issues between the States Parties concerned, and its views on the possibilities of an amicable solution of the matter. This report shall also contain the written submissions and a record of the oral submissions made by the States Parties concerned;

(*d*) If the Commission's report is submitted under subparagraph (*c*), the States Parties concerned shall, within three months of the receipt of the report, notify the Chairman of the Committee whether or not they accept the contents of the report of the Commission.

8. The provisions of this article are without prejudice to the responsibilities of the Committee under article 41.

9. The States Parties concerned shall share equally all the expenses of the members of the Commission in accordance with estimates to be provided by the Secretary-General of the United Nations.

10. The Secretary-General of the United Nations shall be empowered to pay the expenses of the members of the Commission, if necessary, before reimbursement by the States Parties concerned, in accordance with paragraph 9 of this article.

Article 43

The members of the Committee, and of the *ad hoc* conciliation commissions which may be appointed under article 42, shall be entitled to the facilities, privileges and immunities of experts on mission for the United Nations as laid down in the relevant sections of the Convention on the Privileges and Immunities of the United Nations.

Article 44

The provisions for the implementation of the present Covenant shall apply without prejudice to the procedures prescribed in the field of human rights by or under the constituent instruments and the conventions of the United Nations and of the specialized agencies and shall not prevent the States Parties to the present Covenant from having recourse to other procedures for settling a dispute in accordance with general or special international agreements in force between them.

Article 45

The Committee shall submit to the General Assembly of the United Nations, through the Economic and Social Council, an annual report on its activities.

PART V

Article 46

Nothing in the present Covenant shall be interpreted as impairing the provisions of the Charter of the United Nations and of the constitutions of the specialized agencies which define the respective responsibilities of the various organs of the United Nations and of the specialized agencies in regard to the matters dealt with in the present Covenant.

Article 47

Nothing in the present Covenant shall be interpreted as impairing the inherent right of all peoples to enjoy and utilize fully and freely their natural wealth and resources.

PART VI

Article 48

1. The present Covenant is open for signature by any State Member of the United Nations or member of any of its specialized agencies, by any State Party to the Statute of the International Court of Justice, and by any other State which has been invited by the General Assembly of the United Nations to become a Party to the present Covenant.

2. The present Covenant is subject to ratification. Instruments of ratification shall be deposited with the Secretary-General of the United Nations.

3. The present Covenant shall be open to accession by any State referred to in paragraph 1 of this article.

4. Accession shall be effected by the deposit of an instrument of accession with the Secretary-General of the United Nations.

5. The Secretary-General of the United Nations shall inform all States which have signed this Covenant or acceded to it of the deposit of each instrument of ratification or accession.

Article 49

1. The present Covenant shall enter into force three months after the date of the deposit with the Secretary-General of the United Nations of the thirty-fifth instrument of ratification or instrument of accession.

2. For each State ratifying the present Covenant or acceding to it after the deposit of the thirty-fifth instrument of ratification or instrument of accession, the present Covenant shall enter into force three months after the date of the deposit of its own instrument of ratification or instrument of accession.

Article 50

The provisions of the present Covenant shall extend to all parts of federal States without any limitations or exceptions.

Article 51

1. Any State Party to the present Covenant may propose an amendment and file it with the Secretary-General of the United Nations. The Secretary-General of the United Nations shall thereupon communicate any proposed amendments to the States Parties to the present Covenant with a request that they notify him whether they favour a conference of States Parties for the purpose of considering and voting upon the proposals. In the event that at least one third of the States Parties favours such a conference, the Secretary-General shall convene the conference under the auspices of the United Nations. Any amendment adopted by a majority of the States Parties present and voting at the conference shall be submitted to the General Assembly of the United Nations for approval.

2. Amendments shall come into force when they have been approved by the General Assembly of the United Nations and accepted by a two-thirds majority of the States Parties to the present Covenant in accordance with their respective constitutional processes.

3. When amendments come into force, they shall be binding on those States Parties which have accepted them, other States Parties still being bound by the provisions of the present Covenant and any earlier amendment which they have accepted.

Article 52

Irrespective of the notifications made under article 48, paragraph 5, the Secretary-General of the United Nations shall inform all States referred to in paragraph 1 of the same article of the following particulars:

(a) Signatures, ratifications and accessions under article 48;

(b) The date of the entry into force of the present Covenant under article 49 and the date of the entry into force of any amendments under article 51.

Article 53

1. The present Covenant, of which the Chinese, English, French, Russian and Spanish texts are equally authentic, shall be deposited in the archives of the United Nations.

2. The Secretary-General of the United Nations shall transmit certified copies of the present Covenant to all States referred to in article 48.

Optional Protocol to the International Covenant on Civil and Political Rights

Adopted and opened for signature, ratification and accession by General Assembly resolution 2200 A (XXI) of 16 December 1966

ENTRY INTO FORCE: 23 March 1976, in accordance with article 9

The States Parties to the present Protocol,

Considering that in order further to achieve the purposes of the International Covenant on Civil and Political Rights (hereinafter referred to as the Covenant) and the implemenation of its provisions it would be appropriate to enable the Human Rights Committee set up in part IV of the Covenant (hereinafter referred to as the Committee) to receive and consider, as provided in the present Protocol, communications from individuals claiming to be victims of violations of any of the rights set forth in the Covenant,

Have agreed as follows:

Article 1

A State Party to the Covenant that becomes a Party to the present Protocol recognizes the competence of the Committee to receive and consider communciations from individuals subject to its jurisdiction who claim to be victims of a violation by that State Party of any of the rights set forth in the Covenant. No communication shall be received by the Committee if it concerns a State Party to the Covenant which is not a Party to the present Protocol.

Article 2

Subject to the provisions of article 1, individuals who claim that any of their rights enumerated in the Covenant have been violated and who have exhausted all available domestic remedies may submit a written communication to the Committee for consideration.

Article 3

The Committee shall consider inadmissible any communication under the present Protocol which is anonymous, or which it considers to be an abuse of the right of submission of such communciations or to be incompatible with the provisions of the Covenant.

Article 4

1. Subject to the provisions of article 3, the Committee shall bring any communications submitted to it under the present Protocol to the attention of the State Party to the present Protocol alleged to be violating any provision of the Covenant.

2.   Within six months, the receiving State shall submit to the Committee written explanations or statements clarifying the matter and the remedy, if any, that may have been taken by that State.

Article 5

1.   The Committee shall consider communications received under the present Protocol in the light of all written information made available to it by the individual and by the State Party concerned.

2.   The Committee shall not consider any communication from an individual unless it has ascertained that:

(a) The same matter is not being examined under another procedure of international investigation or settlement;

(b) The individual has exhausted all available domestic remedies. This shall not be the rule where the application of the remedies is unreasonably prolonged.

3.   The Committee shall hold closed meetings when examining communications under the present Protocol.

4.   The Committee shall forward its views to the State Party concerned and to the individual.

Article 6

The Committee shall include in its annual report under article 45 of the Covenant a summary of its activities under the present Protocol.

Article 7

Pending the achievement of the objectives of resolution 1514 (XV) adopted by the General Assembly of the United Nations on 14 December 1960 concerning the Declaration on the Granting of Independence to Colonial Countries and Peoples, the provisions of the present Protocol shall in no way limit the right of petition granted to these peoples by the Charter of the United Nations and other international conventions and instruments under the United Nations and its specialized agencies.

Article 8

1.   The present Protocol is open for signature by any State which has signed the Covenant.

2.   The present Protocol is subject to ratification by any State which has ratified or acceded to the Covenant. Instruments of ratification shall be deposited with the Secretary-General of the United Nations.

3.   The present Protocol shall be open to accession by any State which has ratified or acceded to the Covenant.

4.   Accession shall be effected by the deposit of an instrument of accession with the Secretary-General of the United Nations.

5.   The Secretary-General of the United Nations shall inform all States which have signed the present Protocol or acceded to it of the deposit of each instrument of ratification or accession.

Article 9

1.   Subject to the entry into force of the Covenant, the present Protocol shall enter into force three months after the date of the deposit with the Secretary-General of the United Nations of the tenth instrument of ratification or instrument of accession.

2.   For each State ratifying the present Protocol or acceding to it after the deposit of the tenth instrument of ratification or instrument of accession, the present Protocol shall enter into force three months after the date of the deposit of its own instrument of ratification or instrument of accession.

Article 10

The provisions of the present Protocol shall extend to all parts of federal States without any limitations or exceptions.

Article 11

1.   Any State Party to the present Protocol may propose an amendment and file it with the Secretary-General of the United Nations. The Secretary-General shall thereupon communicate any proposed amendments to the States Parties to the present Protocol with a request that they notify him whether they favour a conference of States Parties for the purpose of considering and voting upon the proposal. In the event that at least one third of the States Parties favours such a conference, the Secretary-General shall convene the conference under the auspices of the United Nations. Any amendment adopted by a majority of the States Parties present and voting at the conference shall be submitted to the General Assembly of the United Nations for approval.

2.   Amendments shall come into force when they have been approved by the General Assembly of the United Nations and accepted by a two-thirds majority of the States Parties to the present Protocol in accordance with their respective constitutional processes.

3.   When amendments come into force, they shall be binding on those States Parties which have accepted them, other States Parties still being bound by the provisions of the present Protocol and any earlier amendment which they have accepted.

Article 12

1.   Any State Party may denounce the present Protocol at any time by written notification addressed to the Secretary-General of the United Na-

tions. Denunciation shall take effect three months after the date of receipt of the notification by the Secretary-General.

2.   Denunciation shall be without prejudice to the continued application of the provisions of the present Protocol to any communication submitted under article 2 before the effective date of denunciation.

Article 13

Irrespective of the notifications made under article 8, paragraph 5, of the present Protocol, the Secretary-General of the United Nations shall inform all States referred to in article 48, paragraph 1, of the Covenant of the following particulars:

(a) Signatures, ratifications and accessions under article 8;

(b) The date of the entry into force of the present Protocol under article 9 and the date of the entry into force of any amendments under article 11;

(c) Denunciations under article 12.

Article 14

1.   The present Protocol, of which the Chinese, English, French, Russian and Spanish texts are equally authentic, shall be deposited in the archives of the United Nations.

2.   The Secretary-General of the United Nations shall transmit certified copies of the present Protocol to all States referred to in article 48 of the Covenant.

International Convention on the Elimination of All Forms of Racial Discrimination

Adopted and opened for signature and ratification by General Assembly resolution 2106 A (XX) of 21 December 1965

ENTRY INTO FORCE: 4 January 1969, in accordance with article 19

The States Parties to this Convention,

Considering that the Charter of the United Nations is based on the principles of the dignity and equality inherent in all human beings, and that all Member States have pledged themselves to take joint and separate action, in co-operation with the Organization, for the achievement of one of the purposes of the United Nations which is to promote and encourage universal respect for and observance of human rights and fundamental freedoms for all, without distinction as to race, sex, language or religion,

Considering that the Universal Declaration of Human Rights proclaims that all human beings are born free and equal in dignity and rights and that everyone is entitled to all the rights and freedoms set out therein, without distinction of any kind, in particular as to race, colour or national origin,

Considering that all human beings are equal before the law and are entitled to equal protection of the law against any discrimination and against any incitement to discrimination,

Considering that the United Nations has condemned colonialism and all practices of segregation and discrimination associated therewith, in whatever form and wherever they exist, and that the Declaration on the Granting of Independence to Colonial Countries and Peoples of 14 December 1960 (General Assembly resolution 1514 (XV)) has affirmed and solemnly proclaimed the necessity of bringing them to a speedy and unconditional end,

Considering that the United Nations Declaration on the Elimination of All Forms of Racial Discrimination of 20 November 1963 (General Assembly resolution 1904 (XVIII)) solemnly affirms the necessity of speedily eliminating racial discrimination throughout the world in all its forms and manifestations and of securing understanding of and respect for the dignity of the human person,

Convinced that any doctrine of superiority based on racial differentiation is scientifically false, morally condemnable, socially unjust and dangerous, and that there is no justification for racial discrimination, in theory or in practice, anywhere,

Reaffirming that discrimination between human beings on the grounds of race, colour or ethnic origin is an obstacle to friendly and peaceful relations among nations and is capable of disturbing peace and security among peoples and the harmony of persons living side by side even within one and the same State,

Convinced that the existence of racial barriers is repugnant to the ideals of any human society,

Alarmed by manifestations of racial discrimination still in evidence in some areas of the world and by governmental policies based on racial superiority or hatred, such as policies of *apartheid*, segregation or separation,

Resolved to adopt all necessary measures for speedily eliminating racial discrimination in all its forms and manifestations, and to prevent and combat racist doctrines and practices in order to promote understanding between races and to build an international community free from all forms of racial segregation and racial discrimination,

Bearing in mind the Convention concerning Discrimination in respect of Employment and Occupation adopted by the International Labour Organisation in 1958, and the Convention against Discrimination in Education adopted by the United Nations Educational, Scientific and Cultural Organization in 1960,

Desiring to implement the principles embodied in the United Nations Declaration on the Elimination of All Forms of Racial Discrimination and to secure the earliest adoption of practical measures to that end,

Have agreed as follows:

PART I

Article 1

1. In this Convention, the term "racial discrimination" shall mean any distinction, exclusion, restriction or preference based on race, colour, descent, or national or ethnic origin which has the purpose or effect of nullifying or impairing the recognition, enjoyment or exercise, on an equal footing, of human rights and fundamental freedoms in the political, economic, social, cultural or any other field of public life.

2. This Convention shall not apply to distinctions, exclusions, restrictions or preferences made by a State Party to this Convention between citizens and non-citizens.

3. Nothing in this Convention may be interpreted as affecting in any way the legal provisions of States Parties concerning nationality, citizenship or naturalization, provided that such provisions do not discriminate against any particular nationality.

4. Special measures taken for the sole purpose of securing adequate advancement of certain racial or ethnic groups or individuals requiring such protection as may be necessary in order to ensure such groups or individuals

equal enjoyment or exercise of human rights and fundamental freedoms shall not be deemed racial discrimination, provided, however, that such measures do not, as a consequence, lead to the maintenance of separate rights for different racial groups and that they shall not be continued after the objectives for which they were taken have been achieved.

Article 2

1.   States Parties condemn racial discrimination and undertake to pursue by all appropriate means and without delay a policy of eliminating racial discrimination in all its forms and promoting understanding among all races, and, to this end:

(a) Each State Party undertakes to engage in no act or practice of racial discrimination against persons, groups of persons or institutions and to ensure that all public authorities and public institutions, national and local, shall act in conformity with this obligation;

(b) Each State Party undertakes not to sponsor, defend or support racial discrimination by any persons or organizations;

(c) Each State Party shall take effective measures to review governmental, national and local policies, and to amend, rescind or nullify any laws and regulations which have the effect of creating or perpetuating racial discrimination wherever it exists;

(d) Each State Party shall prohibit and bring to an end, by all appropriate means, including legislation as required by circumstances, racial discrimination by any persons, group or organization;

(e) Each State Party undertakes to encourage, where appropriate, integrationist multiracial organizations and movements and other means of eliminating barriers between races, and to discourage anything which tends to strengthen racial division.

2.   States Parties shall, when the circumstances so warrant, take, in the social, economic, cultural and other fields, special and concrete measures to ensure the adequate development and protection of certain racial groups or individuals belonging to them, for the purpose of guaranteeing them the full and equal enjoyment of human rights and fundamental freedoms. These measures shall in no case entail as a consequence the maintenance of unequal or separate rights for different racial groups after the objectives for which they were taken have been achieved.

Article 3

States Parties particularly condemn racial segregation and *apartheid* and undertake to prevent, prohibit and eradicate all practices of this nature in territories under their jurisdiction.

Article 4

States Parties condemn all propaganda and all organizations which are based on ideas or theories of superiority of one race or group of persons of one colour or ethnic origin, or which attempt to justify or promote racial hatred and discrimination in any form, and undertake to adopt immediate and positive measures designed to eradicate all incitement to, or acts of, such discrimination and, to this end, with due regard to the principles embodied in the Universal Declaration of Human Rights and the rights expressly set forth in article 5 of this Convention, *inter alia:*

(*a*) Shall declare an offence punishable by law all dissemination of ideas based on racial superiority or hatred, incitement to racial discrimination, as well as all acts of violence or incitement to such acts against any race or group of persons of another colour or ethnic origin, and also the provision of any assistance to racist activities, including the financing thereof;

(*b*) Shall declare illegal and prohibit organizations, and also organized and all other propaganda activities, which promote and incite racial discrimination, and shall recognize participation in such organizations or activities as an offence punishable by law;

(*c*) Shall not permit public authorities or public institutions, national or local, to promote or incite racial discrimination.

Article 5

In compliance with the fundamental obligations laid down in article 2 of this Convention, States Parties undertake to prohibit and to eliminate racial discrimination in all its forms and to guarantee the right of everyone, without distinction as to race, colour, or national or ethnic origin, to equality before the law, notably in the enjoyment of the following rights:

(*a*) The right to equal treatment before the tribunals and all other organs administering justice;

(*b*) The right to security of person and protection by the State against violence or bodily harm, whether inflicted by government officials or by any individual group or institution;

(*c*) Political rights, in particular the rights to participate in elections—to vote and to stand for election—on the basis of universal and equal suffrage, to take part in the Government as well as in the conduct of public affairs at any level and to have equal access to public service;

(*d*) Other civil rights, in particular:

(i) The right to freedom of movement and residence within the border of the State;

(ii) The right to leave any country, including one's own, and to return to one's country;

(iii) The right to nationality;

(iv) The right to marriage and choice of spouse;

(v) The right to own property alone as well as in association with others;

(vi) The right to inherit;

(vii) The right to freedom of throught, conscience and religion;

(viii) The right to freedom of opinion and expression;

(ix) The right to freedom of peaceful assembly and association;

(e) Economic, social and cultural rights, in particular:

(i) The rights to work, to free choice of employment, to just and favourable conditions of work, to protection against unemployment, to equal pay for equal work, to just and favourable remuneration;

(ii) The right to form and join trade unions;

(iii) The right to housing;

(iv) The right to public health, medical care, social security and social services;

(v) The right to education and training;

(vi) The right to equal participation in cultural activities;

(f) The right of access to any place or service intended for use by the general public, such as transport, hotels, restaurants, cafés, theatres and parks.

Article 6

States Parties shall assure to everyone within their jurisdiction effective protection and remedies, through the competent national tribunals and other State institutions, against any acts of racial discrimination which violate his human rights and fundamental freedoms contrary to this Convention, as well as the right to seek from such tribunals just and adequate reparation or satisfaction for any damage suffered as a result of such discrimination.

Article 7

States Parties undertake to adopt immediate and effective measures, particularly in the fields of teaching, education, culture and information, with a view to combating prejudices which lead to racial discrimination and to promoting understanding, tolerance and friendship among nations and racial or ethnical groups, as well as to propagating the purposes and principles of the Charter of the United Nations, the Universal Declaration of Human Rights, the United Nations Declaration on the Elimination of All Forms of Racial Discrimination, and this Convention.

PART II

Article 8

1.   There shall be established a Committee on the Elimination of Racial Discrimination (hereinafter referred to as the Committee) consisting of eighteen experts of high moral standing and acknowledged impartiality elected by States Parties from among their nationals, who shall serve in their personal capacity, consideration being given to equitable geographical distribution and to the representation of the different forms of civilization as well as of the principal legal systems.

2.   The members of the Committee shall be elected by secret ballot from a list of persons nominated by the States Parties. Each State Party may nominate one person from among its own nationals.

3.   The initial election shall be held six months after the date of the entry into force of this Convention. At least three months before the date of each election the Secretary-General of the United Nations shall address a letter to the States Parties inviting them to submit their nominations within two months. The Secretary-General shall prepare a list in alphabetical order of all persons thus nominated, indicating the States Parties which have nominated them, and shall submit it to the States Parties.

4.   Elections of the members of the Committee shall be held at a meeting of States Parties convened by the Secretary-General at United Nations Headquarters. At that meeting, for which two thirds of the States Parties shall constitute a quorum, the persons elected to the Committee shall be nominees who obtain the largest number of votes and an absolute majority of the votes of the representatives of States Parties present and voting.

5.   (*a*) The members of the Committee shall be elected for a term of four years. However, the terms of nine of the members elected at the first election shall expire at the end of two years; immediately after the first election the names of these nine members shall be chosen by lot by the Chairman of the Committee;

(*b*) For the filling of casual vacancies, the State Party whose expert has ceased to function as a member of the Committee shall appoint another expert from among its nationals, subject to the approval of the Committee.

6.   States Parties shall be responsible for the expenses of the members of the Committee while they are in performance of Committee duties.

Article 9

1.   States Parties undertake to submit to the Secretary-General of the United Nations, for consideration by the Committee, a report on the legislative, judicial, administrative or other measures which they have adopted and which give effect to the provisions of this Convention: (*a*) within one year after the entry into force of the Convention for the State concerned; and

(b) thereafter every two years and whenever the Committee so requests. The Committee may request further information from the States Parties.

2. The Committee shall report annually, through the Secretary-General, to the General Assembly of the United Nations on its activities and may make suggestions and general recommendations based on the examination of the reports and information received from the States Parties. Such suggestions and general recommendations shall be reported to the General Assembly together with comments, if any, from States Parties.

Article 10

1. The Committee shall adopt its own rules of procedure.

2. The Committee shall elect its officers for a term of two years.

3. The secretariat of the Committee shall be provided by the Secretary-General of the United Nations.

4. The meetings of the Committee shall normally be held at United Nations Headquarters.

Article 11

1. If a State Party considers that another State Party is not giving effect to the provisions of this Convention, it may bring the matter to the attention of the Committee. The Committee shall then transmit the communication to the State Party concerned. Within three months, the receiving State shall submit to the Committee written explanations or statements clarifying the matter and the remedy, if any, that may have been taken by that State.

2. If the matter is not adjusted to the satisfaction of both parties, either by bilateral negotiations or by any other procedure open to them, within six months after the receipt by the receiving State of the initial communication, either State shall have the right to refer the matter again to the Committee by notifying the Committee and also the other State.

3. The Committee shall deal with a matter referred to it in accordance with paragraph 2 of this article after it has ascertained that all available domestic remedies have been invoked and exhausted in the case, in conformity with the generally recognized principles of international law. This shall not be the rule where the application of the remedies is unreasonably prolonged.

4. In any matter referred to it, the Committee may call upon the States Parties concerned to supply any other relevant information.

5. When any matter arising out of this article is being considered by the Committee, the States Parties concerned shall be entitled to send a representative to take part in the proceedings of the Committee, without voting rights, while the matter is under consideration.

Article 12

1. (*a*) After the Committee has obtained and collated all the information it deems necessary, the Chairman shall apppoint an *ad hoc* Conciliation Commission (hereinafter referred to as the Commission) comprising five persons who may or may not be members of the Committee. The members of the Commission shall be appointed with the unanimous consent of the parties to the dispute, and its good offices shall be made available to the States concerned with a view to an amicable solution of the matter on the basis of respect for this Convention;

(*b*) If the States parties to the dispute fail to reach agreement within three months on all or part of the composition of the Commission, the members of the Commission not agreed upon by the States parties to the dispute shall be elected by secret ballot by a two-thirds majority vote of the Committee from among its own members.

2. The members of the Commission shall serve in their personal capacity. They shall not be nationals of the States parties to the dispute or of a State not Party to this Convention.

3. The Commission shall elect its own Chairman and adopt its own rules of procedure.

4. The meetings of the Commission shall normally be held at United Nations Headquarters or at any other convenient place as determined by the Commission.

5. The secretariat provided in accordance with article 10, paragraph 3, of this Convention shall also service the Commission whenever a dispute among States Parties brings the Commission into being.

6. The States parties to the dispute shall share equally all the expenses of the members of the Commission in accordance with estimates to be provided by the Secretary-General of the United Nations.

7. The Secretary-General shall be empowered to pay the expenses of the members of the Commission, if necessary, before reimbursement by the States parties to the dispute in accordance with paragraph 6 of this article.

8. The information obtained and collated by the Committee shall be made available to the Commission, and the Commission may call upon the States concerned to supply any other relevant information.

Article 13

1. When the Commission has fully considered the matter, it shall prepare and submit to the Chairman of the Committe a report embodying its findings on all questions of fact relevant to the issue between the parties and containing such recommendations as it may think proper for the amicable solution of the dispute.

2. The Chairman of the Committee shall communicate the report of the Commission to each of the States parties to the dispute. These States shall, within three months, inform the Chairman of the Committee whether or not they accept the recommendations contained in the report of the Commission.

3. After the period provided for in paragraph 2 of this article, the Chairman of the Committee shall communicate the report of the Commission and the declarations of the States Parties concerned to the other States Parties to this Convention.

Article 14

1. A State Party may at any time declare that it recognizes the competence of the Committee to receive and consider communications from individuals or groups of individuals within its jurisdiction claiming to be victims of a violation by that State Party of any of the rights set forth in this Convention. No communication shall be received by the Committee if it concerns a State Party which has not made such a declaration.

2. Any State Party which makes a declaration as provided for in paragraph 1 of this article may establish or indicate a body within its national legal order which shall be competent to receive and consider petitions from individuals and groups of individuals within its jurisdiction who claim to be victims of a violation of any of the rights set forth in this Convention and who have exhausted other available local remedies.

3. A declaration made in accordance with paragraph 1 of this article and the name of any body established or indicated in accordance with paragraph 2 of this article shall be deposited by the State Party concerned with the Secretary-General of the United Nations, who shall transmit copies thereof to the other States Parties. A declaration may be withdrawn at any time by notification to the Secretary-General, but such a withdrawal shall not affect communications pending before the Committee.

4. A register of petitions shall be kept by the body established or indicated in accordance with paragraph 2 of this article, and certified copies of the register shall be filed annually through appropriate channels with the Secretary-General on the understanding that the contents shall not be publicly disclosed.

5. In the event of failure to obtain satisfaction from the body established or indicated in accordance with paragraph 2 of this article, the petitioner shall have the right to communicate the matter to the Committee within six months.

6. (a) The Committee shall confidentially bring any communication referred to it to the attention of the State Party alleged to be violating any provision of this Convention, but the identity of the individual or groups of

individuals concerned shall not be revealed without his or their express consent. The Committee shall not receive anonymous communications;

(b) Within three months, the receiving State shall submit to the Committee written explanations or statements clarifying the matter and the remedy, if any, that may have been taken by that State.

7. (a) The Committee shall consider communications in the light of all information made available to it by the State Party concerned and by the petitioner. The Committee shall not consider any communication from a petitioner unless it has ascertained that the petitioner has exhausted all available domestic remedies. However, this shall not be the rule where the application of the remedies is unreasonably prolonged;

(b) The Committee shall forward its suggestions and recommendations, if any, to the State Party concerned and to the petitioner.

8. The Committee shall include in its annual report a summary of such communications and, where appropriate, a summary of the explanations and statements of the States Parties concerned and of its own suggestions and recommendations.

9. The Committee shall be competent to exercise the functions provided for in this article only when at least ten States Parties to this Convention are bound by declarations in accordance with paragraph 1 of this article.

Article 15

1. Pending the achievement of the objectives of the Declaration on the Granting of Independence to Colonial Countries and Peoples, contained in General Assembly resolution 1514 (XV) of 14 December 1960, the provisions of this Convention shall in no way limit the right of petition granted to these peoples by other international instruments or by the United Nations and its specialized agencies.

2. (a) The Committee established under article 8, paragraph 1, of this Convention shall receive copies of the petitions from, and submit expressions of opinion and recommendations on these petitions to, the bodies of the United Nations which deal with matters directly related to the principles and objectives of this Convention in their consideration of petitions from the inhabitants of Trust and Non-Self-Governing Territories and all other territories to which General Assembly resolution 1514 (XV) applies, relating to matters covered by this Convention which are before these bodies;

(b) The Committee shall receive from the competent bodies of the United Nations copies of the reports concerning the legislative, judicial, administrative or other measures directly related to the principles and objectives of this Convention applied by the administering Powers within the Territories mentioned in subparagraph (a) of this paragraph, and shall express opinions and make recommendations to these bodies.

3.   The Committee shall include in its report to the General Assembly a summary of the petitions and reports it has received from United Nations bodies, and the expressions of opinion and recommendations of the Committee relating to the said petitions and reports.

4.   The Committee shall request from the Secretary-General of the United Nations all information relevant to the objectives of this Convention and available to him regarding the Territories mentioned in paragraph 2 (a) of this article.

Article 16

The provisions of this Convention concerning the settlement of disputes or complaints shall be applied without prejudice to other procedures for settling disputes or complaints in the field of discrimination laid down in the constituent instruments of, or conventions adopted by, the United Nations and its specialized agencies, and shall not prevent the States Parties from having recourse to other procedures for settling a dispute in accordance with general or special international agreements in force between them.

PART III

Article 17

1.   This Convention is open for signature by any State Member of the United Nations or member of any of its specialized agencies, by any State Party to the Statute of the International Court of Justice, and by any other State which has been invited by the General Assembly of the United Nations to become a Party to this Convention.

2.   This Convention is subject to ratification. Instruments of ratification shall be deposited with the Secretary-General of the United Nations.

Article 18

1.   This Convention shall be open to accession by any State referred to in article 17, paragraph 1, of the Convention.

2.   Accession shall be effected by the deposit of an instrument of accession with the Secretary-General of the United Nations.

Article 19

1.   This Convention shall enter into force on the thirtieth day after the date of the deposit with the Secretary-General of the United Nations of the twenty-seventh instrument of ratification or instrument of accession.

2.   For each State ratifying this Convention or acceding to it after the deposit of the twenty-seventh instrument of ratification or instrument of accession, the Convention shall enter into force on the thirtieth day after the date of the deposit of its own instrument of ratification or instrument of accession.

Article 20

1.   The Secretary-General of the United Nations shall receive and circulate to all States which are or may become Parties to this Convention reservations made by States at the time of ratification or accession. Any State which objects to the reservation shall, within a period of ninety days from the date of the said communication, notify the Secretary-General that it does not accept it.

2.   A reservation incompatible with the object and purpose of this Convention shall not be permitted, nor shall a reservation the effect of which would inhibit the operation of any of the bodies established by this Convention be allowed. A reservation shall be considered incompatible or inhibitive if at least two thirds of the States Parties to this Convention object to it.

3.   Reservations may be withdrawn at any time by notification to this effect addressed to the Secretary-General. Such notification shall take effect on the date on which it is received.

Article 21

A State Party may denounce this Convention by written notification to the Secretary-General of the United Nations. Denunciation shall take effect one year after the date of receipt of the notification by the Secretary-General.

Article 22

Any dispute between two or more States Parties with respect to the interpretation or application of this Convention, which is not settled by negotiation or by the procedures expressly provided for in this Convention, shall, at the request of any of the parties to the dispute, be referred to the International Court of Justice for decision, unless the disputants agree to another mode of settlement.

Article 23

1.   A request for the revision of this Convention may be made at any time by any State Party by means of a notification in writing addressed to the Secretary-General of the United Nations.

2.   The General Assembly of the United Nations shall decide upon the steps, if any, to be taken in respect of such a request.

Article 24

The Secretary-General of the United Nations shall inform all States referred to in article 17, paragraph 1, of this Convention of the following particulars:

(*a*) Signatures, ratifications and accessions under articles 17 and 18;

(*b*) The date of entry into force of this Convention under article 19;

(*c*) Communications and declarations received under articles 14, 20 and 23;

(*d*) Denunciations under article 21.

Article 25

1. This Convention, of which the Chinese, English, French, Russian and Spanish texts are equally authentic, shall be deposited in the archives of the United Nations.

2. The Secretary-General of the United Nations shall transmit certified copies of this Convention to all States belonging to any of the categories mentioned in article 17, paragraph 1, of the Convention.

Convention on the Prevention and Punishment of the Crime of Genocide

Approved and proposed for signature and ratification or accession by General Assembly resolution 260 A (III) of 9 December 1948

ENTRY INTO FORCE: 12 January 1951, in accordance with article XIII

The Contracting Parties,

Having considered the declaration made by the General Assembly of the United Nations in its resolution 96 (I) dated 11 December 1946 that genocide is a crime under international law, contrary to the spirit and aims of the United Nations and condemned by the civilized world,

Recognizing that at all periods of history genocide has inflicted great losses on humanity, and

Being convinced that, in order to liberate mankind from such an odious scourge, international co-operation is required,

Hereby agree as hereinafter provided:

Article I

The Contracting Parties confirm that genocide, whether committed in time of peace or in time of war, is a crime under international law which they undertake to prevent and to punish.

Article II

In the present Convention, genocide means any of the following acts committed with intent to destroy, in whole or in part, a national, ethnical, racial or religious group, as such:

(*a*) Killing members of the group;

(*b*) Causing serious bodily or mental harm to members of the group;

(*c*) Deliberately inflicting on the group conditions of life calculated to bring about its physical destruction in whole or in part;

(*d*) Imposing measures intended to prevent births within the group;

(*e*) Forcibly transferring children of the group to another group.

Article III

The following acts shall be punishable:

(*a*) Genocide;

(*b*) Conspiracy to commit gneocide;

(*c*) Direct and public incitement to commit genocide;

(*d*) Attempt to commit genocide;

(*e*) Complicity in genocide.

Article IV

Persons committing genocide or any of the other acts enumerated in article III shall be punished, whether they are constitutionally responsible rulers, public officials or private individuals.

Article V

The Contracting Parties undertake to enact, in accordance with their respective Constitutions, the necessary legislation to give effect to the provisions of the present Convention, and, in particular, to provide effective penalties for persons guilty of genocide or any of the other acts enumerated in article III.

Article VI

Persons charged with genocide or any of the other acts enumerated in article III shall be tried by a competent tribunal of the State in the territory of which the act was committed, or by such international penal tribunal as may have jurisdiction with respect to those Contracting Parties which shall have accepted its jurisdiction.

Article VII

Genocide and the other acts enumerated in article III shall not be considered as political crimes for the purpose of extradition.

The Contracting Parties pledge themselves in such cases to grant extradition in accordance with their laws and treaties in force.

Article VIII

Any Contracting Party may call upon the competent organs of the United Nations to take such action under the Charter of the United Nations as they consider appropriate for the prevention and suppression of acts of genocide or any of the other acts enumerated in article III.

Article IX

Disputes between the Contracting Parties relating to the interpretation, application or fulfilment of the present Convention, including those relating to the responsibility of a State for genocide or for any of the other acts enumerated in article III, shall be submitted to the International Court of Justice at the request of any of the parties to the dispute.

Article X

The present Convention, of which the Chinese, English, French, Russian and Spanish texts are equally authentic, shall bear the date of 9 December 1948.

Article XI

The present Convention shall be open until 31 December 1949 for signature on behalf of any Member of the United Nations and of any non-member State to which an invitation to sign has been addressed by the General Assembly.

The present Convention shall be ratified, and the instruments of ratification shall be deposited with the Secretary-General of the United Nations.

After 1 January 1950, the present Convention may be acceded to on behalf of any Member of the United Nations and of any non-member State which has received an invitation as aforesaid.

Instruments of accession shall be deposited with the Secretary-General of the United Nations.

Article XII

Any Contracting Party may at any time, by notification addressed to the Secretary-General of the United Nations, extend the application of the present Convention to all or any of the territories for the conduct of whose foreign relations that Contracting Party is responsible.

Article XIII

On the day when the first twenty instruments of ratification or accession have been deposited, the Secretary-General shall draw up a *procès-verbal* and transmit a copy thereof to each Member of the United Nations and to each of the non-member States contemplated in article XI.

The present Convention shall come into force on the ninetieth day following the date of deposit of the twentieth instrument of ratification or accession.

Any ratification or accession effected, subsequent to the latter date shall become effective on the ninetieth day following the deposit of the instrument of ratification or accession.

Article XIV

The present Convention shall remain in effect for a period of ten years as from the date of its coming into force.

It shall thereafter remain in force for successive periods of five years for such Contracting Parties as have not denounced it at least six months before the expiration of the current period.

Denunciation shall be effected by a written notification addressed to the Secretary-General of the United Nations.

Article XV

If, as a result of denunciations, the number of Parties to the present Convention should become less than sixteen, the Convention shall cease to be in force as from the date on which the last of these denunciations shall become effective.

Article XVI

A request for the revision of the present Convention may be made at any time by any Contracting Party by means of a notification in writing addressed to the Secretary-General.

The General Assembly shall decide upon the steps, if any, to be taken in respect of such request.

Article XVII

The Secretary-General of the United Nations shall notify all Members of the United Nations and the non-member States contemplated in article XI of the following:

(a) Signatures, ratifications and accessions received in accordance with article XI;

(b) Notifications received in accordance with article XII;

(c) The date upon which the present Convention comes into force in accordance with article XIII;

(d) Denunciations received in accordance with article XIV;

(e) The abrogation of the Convention in accordance with article XV;

(f) Notifications received in accordance with article XVI.

Article XVIII

The original of the present Convention shall be deposited in the archives of the United Nations.

A certified copy of the Convention shall be transmitted to each Member of the United Nations and to each of the non-member States contemplated in article XI.

Article XIX

The present Convention shall be registered by the Secretary-General of the United Nations on the date of its coming into force.

Standard Minimum Rules for the Treatment of Prisoners

Adopted by the First United Nations Congress on the Prevention of Crime and the Treatment of Offenders, held at Geneva in 1955, and approved by the Economic and Social Council by its resolutions 663 C (XXIV) of 31 July 1957 and 2076 (LXII) of 13 May 1977

PRELIMINARY OBSERVATIONS

1. The following rules are not intended to describe in detail a model system of penal institutions. They seek only, on the basis of the general consensus of contemporary thought and the essential elements of the most adequate systems of today, to set out what is generally accepted as being good principle and practice in the treatment of prisoners and the management of institutions.

2. In view of the great variety of legal, social, economic and geographical conditions of the world, it is evident that not all of the rules are capable of application in all places and at all times. They should, however, serve to stimulate a constant endeavour to overcome practical difficulties in the way of their application, in the knowledge that they represent, as a whole, the minimum conditions which are accepted as suitable by the United Nations.

3. On the other hand, the rules cover a field in which thought is constantly developing. They are not intended to preclude experiment and practices, provided these are in harmony with the principles and seek to further the purposes which derive from the text of the rules as a whole. It will always be justifiable for the central prison administration to authorize departures from the rules in this spirit.

4. (1) Part I of the rules covers the general management of institutions, and is applicable to all categories of prisoners, criminal or civil, untried or convicted, including prisoners subject to "security measures" or corrective measures ordered by the judge.

(2) Part II contains rules applicable only to tne special categories dealt with in each section. Nevertheless, the rules under section A, applicable to prisoners under sentence, shall be equally applicable to categories of prisoners dealt with in sections B, C and D, provided they do not conflict with the rules governing those categories and are for their benefit.

5. (1) The rules do not seek to regulate the management of institutions set aside for young persons such as Borstal institutions or

correctional schools, but in general part I would be equally applicable in such institutions.

(2) The category of young prisoners should include at least all young persons who come within the jurisdiction of juvenile courts. As a rule, such young persons should not be sentenced to imprisonment.

PART I

RULES OF GENERAL APPLICATION

Basic principle

6. (1) The following rules shall be applied impartially. There shall be no discrimination on grounds of race, colour, sex, language, religion, political or other opinion, national or social origin, property, birth or other status.

(2) On the other hand, it is necessary to respect the religious beliefs and moral precepts of the group to which a prisoner belongs.

Register

7. (1) In every place where persons are imprisoned there shall be kept a bound registration book with numbered pages in which shall be entered in respect of each prisoner received:

(*a*) Information concerning his identity;

(*b*) The reasons for his commitment and the authority therefor;

(*c*) The day and hour of his admission and release.

(2) No person shall be received in an institution without a valid commitment order of which the details shall have been previously entered in the register.

Separation of categories

8. The different categories of prisoners shall be kept in separate institutions or parts of institutions taking account of their sex, age, criminal record, the legal reason for their detention and the necessities of their treatment. Thus,

(*a*) Men and women shall so far as possible be detained in separate institutions: in an institution which receives both men and women the whole of the premises allocated to women shall be entirely separate;

(*b*) Untried prisoners shall be kept separate from convicted prisoners;

(*c*) Persons imprisoned for debt and other civil prisoners shall be kept separate from persons imprisoned by reason of a criminal offence;

(*d*) Young prisoners shall be kept separate from adults.

Accommodation

9. (1) Where sleeping accommodation is in individual cells or rooms, each prisoner shall occupy by night a cell or room by himself. If for special reasons, such as temporary overcrowding, it becomes necessary for the central prison administration to make an exception to this rule, it is not desirable to have two prisoners in a cell or room.

(2) Where dormitories are used, they shall be occupied by prisoners carefully selected as being suitable to associate with one another in those conditions. There shall be regular supervision by night, in keeping with the nature of the institution.

10. All accommodation provided for the use of prisoners and in particular all sleeping accommodation shall meet all requirements of health, due regard being paid to climatic conditions and particularly to cubic content of air, minimum floor space, lighting, heating and ventilation.

11. In all places where prisoners are required to live or work,

(a) The windows shall be large enough to enable the prisoners to read or work by natural light, and shall be so constructed that they can allow the entrance of fresh air whether or not there is artificial ventilation;

(b) Artificial light shall be provided sufficient for the prisoners to read or work without injury to eyesight.

12. The sanitary installations shall be adequate to enable every prisoner to comply with the needs of nature when necessary and in a clean and decent manner.

13. Adequate bathing and shower installations shall be provided so that every prisoner may be enabled and required to have a bath or shower, at a temperature suitable to the climate, as frequently as necessary for general hygiene according to season and geographical region, but at least once a week in a temperate climate.

14. All parts of an institution regularly used by prisoners shall be properly maintained and kept scrupulously clean at all times.

Personal hygiene

15. Prisoners shall be required to keep their persons clean, and to this end they shall be provided with water and with such toilet articles as are necessary for health and cleanliness.

16. In order that prisoners may maintain a good appearance compatible with their self-respect, facilities shall be provided for the proper care of the hair and beard, and men shall be enabled to shave regularly.

Clothing and bedding

17. (1) Every prisoner who is not allowed to wear his own clothing shall be provided with an outfit of clothing suitable for the climate and adequate to

keep him in good health. Such clothing shall in no manner be degrading or humiliating.

(2) All clothing shall be clean and kept in proper condition. Under-clothing shall be changed and washed as often as necessary for the maintenance of hygiene.

(3) In exceptional circumstances, whenever a prisoner is removed outside the institution for an authorized purpose, he shall be allowed to wear his own clothing or other inconspicuous clothing.

18. If prisoners are allowed to wear their own clothing, arrangements shall be made on their admission to the institution to ensure that it shall be clean and fit for use.

19. Every prisoner shall, in accordance with local or national standards, be provided with a separate bed, and with separate and sufficient bedding which shall be clean when issued, kept in good order and changed often enough to ensure its cleanliness.

Food

20. (1) Every prisoner shall be provided by the administration at the usual hours with food of nutritional value adequate for health and strength, of wholesome quality and well prepared and served.

(2) Drinking water shall be available to every prisoner whenever he needs it.

Exercise and sport

21. (1) Every prisoner who is not employed in outdoor work shall have at least one hour of suitable exercise in the open air daily if the weather permits.

(2) Young prisoners, and others of suitable age and physique, shall receive physical and recreational training during the period of exercise. To this end space, installations and equipment should be provided.

Medical services

22. (1) At every institution there shall be available the services of at least one qualified medical officer who should have some knowledge of psychiatry. The medical services should be organized in close relationship to the general health administration of the community or nation. They shall include a psychiatric service for the diagnosis and, in proper cases, the treatment of states of mental abnormality.

(2) Sick prisoners who require specialist treatment shall be transferred to specialized institutions or to civil hospitals. Where hospital facilities are provided in an institution, their equipment, furnishings and pharmaceutical

supplies shall be proper for the medical care and treatment of sick prisoners, and there shall be a staff of suitable trained officers.

(3) The services of a qualified dental officer shall be available to every prisoner.

23.   (1) In women's institutions there shall be special accommodation for all necessary pre-natal and post-natal care and treatment. Arrangements shall be made wherever practicable for children to be born in a hospital outside the institution. If a child is born in prison, this fact shall not be mentioned in the birth certificate.

(2) Where nursing infants are allowed to remain in the institution with their mothers, provision shall be made for a nursery staffed by qualified persons, where the infants shall be placed when they are not in the care of their mothers.

24.   The medical officer shall see and examine every prisoner as soon as possible after his admission and thereafter as necessary, with a view particularly to the discovery of physical or mental illness and the taking of all necessary measures: the segregation of prisoners suspected of infectious or contagious conditions; the noting of physical or mental defects which might hamper rehabilitation, and the determination of the physical capacity of every prisoner for work.

25.   (1) The medical officer shall have the care of the physical and mental health of the prisoners and should daily see all sick prisoners, all who complain of illness, and any prisoner to whom his attention is specially directed.

(2) The medical officer shall report to the director whenever he considers that a prisoner's physical or mental health has been or will be injuriously affected by continued imprisonment or by any condition of imprisonment.

26.   (1) The medical officer shall regularly inspect and advise the director upon:

(*a*) The quantity, quality, preparation and service of food;

(*b*) The hygiene and cleanliness of the institution and the prisoners;

(*c*) The sanitation, heating, lighting and ventilation of the institution;

(*d*) The suitability and cleanliness of the prisoners' clothing and bedding;

(*e*) The observance of the rules concerning physical education and sports, in cases where there is no technical personnel in charge of these activities.

(2) The director shall take into consideration the reports and advice that the medical officer submits according to rules 25 (2) and 26 and, in case he concurs with the recommendations made, shall take immediate steps to give effect to those recommendations; if they are not within his competence or if

he does not concur with them, he shall immediately submit his own report and the advice of the medical officer to higher authority.

Discipline and punishment

27. Discipline and order shall be maintained with firmness, but with no more restriction than is necessary for safe custody and well-ordered community life.

28. (1) No prisoner shall be employed, in the service of the institution, in any disciplinary capacity.

(2) This rule shall not, however, impede the proper functioning of systems based on self-government, under which specified social, educational or sports activities or responsibilities are entrusted, under supervision, to prisoners who are formed into groups for the purposes of treatment.

29. The following shall always be determined by the law or by the regulation of the competent administrative authority:

(a) Conduct constituting a disciplinary offence;

(b) The types and duration of punishment which may be inflicted;

(c) The authority competent to impose such punishment.

30. (1) No prisoner shall be punished except in accordance with the terms of such law or regulation, and never twice for the same offence.

(2) No prisoner shall be punished unless he has been informed of the offence alleged against him and given a proper opportunity of presenting his defence. The competent authority shall conduct a thorough examination of the case.

(3) Where necessary and practicable the prisoner shall be allowed to make his defence through an interpreter.

31. Corporal punishment, punishment by placing in a dark cell, and all cruel, inhuman or degrading punishments shall be completely prohibited as punishments for disciplinary offences.

32. (1) Punishment by close confinement or reduction of diet shall never be inflicted unless the medical officer has examined the prisoner and certified in writing that he is fit to sustain it.

(2) The same shall apply to any other punishment that may be prejudicial to the physical or mental health of a prisoner. In no case may such punishment be contrary to or depart from the principle stated in rule 31.

(3) The medical officer shall visit daily prisoners undergoing such punishments and shall advise the director if he considers the termination or alteration of the punishment necessary on grounds of physical or mental health.

Instruments of restraint

33.   Instruments of restraint, such as handcuffs, chains, irons and strait-jackets, shall never be applied as a punishment. Furthermore, chains or irons shall not be used as restraints. Other instruments of restraint shall not be used except in the following circumstances:

(*a*) As a precaution against escape during a transfer, provided that they shall be removed when the prisoner appears before a judicial or administrative authority;

(*b*) On medical grounds by direction of the medical officer;

(*c*) By order of the director, if other methods of control fail, in order to prevent a prisoner from injuring himself or others or from damaging property; in such instances the director shall at once consult the medical officer and report to the higher administrative authority.

34.   The patterns and manner of use of instruments of restraint shall be decided by the central prison administration. Such instruments must not be applied for any longer time than is strictly necessary.

Information to and complaints by prisoners

35.   (1) Every prisoner on admission shall be provided with written information about the regulations governing the treatment of prisoners of his category, the disciplinary requirements of the institution, the authorized methods of seeking information and making complaints, and all such other matters as are necessary to enable him to understand both his rights and his obligations and to adapt himself to the life of the institution.

(2) If a prisoner is illiterate, the aforesaid information shall be conveyed to him orally.

36.   (1) Every prisoner shall have the opportunity each week day of making requests or complaints to the director of the institution or the officer authorized to represent him.

(2) It shall be possible to make requests or complaints to the inspector of prisons during his inspection. The prisoner shall have the opportunity to talk to the inspector or to any other inspecting officer without the director or other members of the staff being present.

(3) Every prisoner shall be allowed to make a request or complaint, without censorship as to substance but in proper form, to the central prison administration, the judicial authority or other proper authorities through approved channels.

(4) Unless it is evidently frivolous or groundless, every request or complaint shall be promptly dealt with and replied to without undue delay.

Contact with the outside world

37. Prisoners shall be allowed under necessary supervision to communicate with their family and reputable friends at regular intervals, both by correspondence and by receiving visits.

38. (1) Prisoners who are foreign nationals shall be allowed reasonable facilities to communicate with the diplomatic and consular representatives of the State to which they belong.

(2) Prisoners who are nationals of States without diplomatic or consular representation in the country and refugees or stateless persons shall be allowed similar facilities to communicate with the diplomatic representative of the State which takes charge of their interests or any national or international authority whose task it is to protect such persons.

39. Prisoners shall be kept informed regularly of the more important items of news by the reading of newspapers, periodicals or special institutional publications, by hearing wireless transmissions, by lectures or by any similar means as authorized or controlled by the administration.

Books

40. Every institution shall have a library for the use of all categories of prisoners, adequately stocked with both recreational and instructional books, and prisoners shall be encouraged to make full use of it.

Religion

41. (1) If the institution contains a sufficient number of prisoners of the same religion, a qualified representative of that religion shall be appointed or approved. If the number of prisoners justifies it and conditions permit, the arrangement should be on a full-time basis.

(2) A qualified representative appointed or approved under paragraph (1) shall be allowed to hold regular services and to pay pastoral visits in private to prisoners of his religion at proper times.

(3) Access to a qualified representative of any religion shall not be refused to any prisoner. On the other hand, if any prisoner should object to a visit of any religious representative, his attitude shall be fully respected.

42. So far as practicable, every prisoner shall be allowed to satisfy the needs of his religious life by attending the services provided in the institution and having in his possession the books of religious observance and instruction of his denomination.

Retention of prisoners' property

43. (1) All money, valuables, clothing and other effects belonging to a prisoner which under the regulations of the institution he is not allowed to retain shall on his admission to the institution be placed in safe custody. An

inventory thereof shall be signed by the prisoner. Steps shall be taken to keep them in good condition.

(2) On the release of the prisoner all such articles and money shall be returned to him except in so far as he has been authorized to spend money or send any such property out of the institution, or it has been found necessary on hygienic grounds to destroy any article of clothing. The prisoner shall sign a receipt for the articles and money returned to him.

(3) Any money or effects received for a prisoner from outside shall be treated in the same way.

(4) If a prisoner brings in any drugs or medicine, the medical officer shall decide what use shall be made of them.

Notification of death, illness, transfer, etc.

44. (1) Upon the death or serious illness of, or serious injury to a prisoner, or his removal to an institution for the treatment of mental affections, the director shall at once inform the spouse, if the prisoner is married, or the nearest relative and shall in any event inform any other person previously designated by the prisoner.

(2) A prisoner shall be informed at once of the death or serious illness of any near relative. In case of the critical illness of a near relative, the prisoner should be authorized, whenever circumstances allow, to go to his bedside either under escort or alone.

(3) Every prisoner shall have the right to inform at once his family of his imprisonment or his transfer to another institution.

Removal of prisoners

45. (1) When the prisoners are being removed to or from an institution, they shall be exposed to public view as little as possible, and proper safeguards shall be adopted to protect them from insult, curiosity and publicity in any form.

(2) The transport of prisoners in conveyances with inadequate ventilation or light, or in any way which would subject them to unnecessary physical hardship, shall be prohibited.

(3) The transport of prisoners shall be carried out at the expense of the administration and equal conditions shall obtain for all of them.

Institutional personnel

46. (1) The prison administration, shall provide for the careful selection of every grade of the personnel, since it is on their integrity, humanity, professional capacity and personal suitability for the work that the proper administration of the institutions depends.

(2) The prison administration shall constantly seek to awaken and maintain in the minds both of the personnel and of the public the conviction that this work is a social service of great importance, and to this end all appropriate means of informing the public should be used.

(3) To secure the foregoing ends, personnel shall be appointed on a full-time basis as professional prison officers and have civil service status with security of tenure subject only to good conduct, efficiency and physical fitness. Salaries shall be adequate to attract and retain suitable men and women; employment benefits and conditions of service shall be favourable in view of the exacting nature of the work.

47. (1) The personnel shall possess an adequate standard of education and intelligence.

(2) Before entering on duty, the personnel shall be given a course of training in their general and specific duties and be required to pass theoretical and practical tests.

(3) After entering on duty and during their career, the personnel shall maintain and improve their knowledge and professional capacity by attending courses of in-service training to be organized at suitable intervals.

48. All members of the personnel shall at all times so conduct themselves and perform their duties as to influence the prisoners for good by their example and to command their respect.

49. (1) So far as possible, the personnel shall include a sufficient number of specialists such as psychiatrists, psychologists, social workers, teachers and trade instructors.

(2) The services of social workers, teachers and trade instructors shall be secured on a permanent basis, without thereby excluding part-time or voluntary workers.

50. (1) The director of an institution should be adequately qualified for his task by character, administrative ability, suitable training and experience.

(2) He shall devote his entire time to his official duties and shall not be appointed on a part-time basis.

(3) He shall reside on the premises of the institution or in its immediate vicinity.

(4) When two or more institutions are under the authority of one director, he shall visit each of them at frequent intervals. A responsible resident official shall be in charge of each of these institutions.

51. (1) The director, his deputy, and the majority of the other personnel of the institution shall be able to speak the language of the greatest number of prisoners, or a language understood by the greatest number of them.

(2) Whenever necessary, the services of an interpreter shall be used.

52.   (1) In institutions which are large enough to require the services of one or more full-time medical officers, at least one of them shall reside on the premises of the institution or in its immediate vicinity.

(2) In other institutions the medical officer shall visit daily and shall reside near enough to be able to attend without delay in cases of urgency.

53.   (1) In an institution for both men and women, the part of the institution set aside for women shall be under the authority of a responsible woman officer who shall have the custody of the keys of all that part of the institution.

(2) No male member of the staff shall enter the part of the institution set aside for women unless accompanied by a woman officer.

(3) Women prisoners shall be attended and supervised only by women officers. This does not, however, preclude male members of the staff, particularly doctors and teachers, from carrying out their professional duties in institutions or parts of institutions set aside for women.

54.   (1) Officers of the institutions shall not, in their relations with the prisoners, use force except in self-defence or in cases of attempted escape, or active or passive physical resistance to an order based on law or regulations. Officers who have recourse to force must use no more than is strictly necessary and must report the incident immediately to the director of the institution.

(2) Prison officers shall be given special physical training to enable them to restrain aggressive prisoners.

(3) Except in special circumstances, staff performing duties which bring them into direct contact with prisoners should not be armed. Furthermore, staff should in no circumstances be provided with arms unless they have been trained in their use.

Inspection

55.   There shall be a regular inspection of penal institutions and services by qualified and experienced inspectors appointed by a competent authority. Their task shall be in particular to ensure that these institutions are administered in accordance with existing laws and regulations and with a view to bringing about the objectives of penal and correctional services.

PART II

RULES APPLICABLE TO SPECIAL CATEGORIES

A. PRISONERS UNDER SENTENCE

Guiding principles

56.   The guiding principles hereafter are intended to show the spirit in which penal institutions should be administered and the purposes at which

they should aim, in accordance with the declaration made under Preliminary Observation 1 of the present text.

57.   Imprisonment and other measures which result in cutting off an offender from the outside world are afflictive by the very fact of taking from the person the right of self-determination by depriving him of his liberty. Therefore the prison system shall not, except as incidental to justifiable segregation or the maintenance of discipline, aggravate the suffering inherent in such a situation.

58.   The purpose and justification of a sentence of imprisonment or a similar measure deprivative of liberty is ultimately to protect society against crime. This end can only be achieved if the period of imprisonment is used to ensure, so far as possible, that upon his return to society the offender is not only willing but able to lead a law-abiding and self-supporting life.

59.   To this end, the institution should utilize all the remedial, educational, moral, spiritual and other forces and forms of assistance which are appropriate and available, and should seek to apply them according to the individual treatment needs of the prisoners.

60.   (1) The régime of the institution should seek to minimize any differences betwen prison life and life at liberty which tend to lessen the responsibility of the prisoners or the respect due to their dignity as human beings.

(2) Before the completion of the sentence, it is desirable that the necessary steps be taken to ensure for the prisoner a gradual return to life in society. This aim may be achieved, depending on the case, by a pre-release régime organized in the same institution or in another appropriate institution, or by release on trial under some kind of supervision which must not be entrusted to the police but should be combined with effective social aid.

61.   The treatment of prisoners should emphasize not their exclusion from the community, but their continuing part in it. Community agencies should, therefore, be enlisted wherever possible to assist the staff of the institution in the task of social rehabilitation of the prisoners. There should be in connection with every institution social workers charged with the duty of maintaining and improving all desirable relations of a prisoner with his family and with valuable social agencies. Steps should be taken to safeguard, to the maximum extent compatible with the law and the sentence, the rights relating to civil interests, social security rights and other social benefits of prisoners.

62.   The medical services of the institution shall seek to detect and shall treat any physical or mental illnesses or defects which may hamper a prisoner's rehabilitation. All necessary medical, surgical and psychiatric services shall be provided to that end.

63. (1) The fulfilment of these principles requires individualization of treatment and for this purpose a flexible system of classifying prisoners in groups; it is therefore desirable that such groups should be distributed in separate institutions suitable for the treatment of each group.

(2) These institutions need not provide the same degree of security for every group. It is desirable to provide varying degrees of security according to the needs of different groups. Open institutions, by the very fact that they provide no physical security against escape but rely on the self-discipline of the inmates, provide the conditions most favourable to rehabilitation for carefully selected prisoners.

(3) It is desirable that the number of prisoners in closed institutions should not be so large that the individualization of treatment is hindered. In some countries it is considered that the population of such institutions should not exceed five hundred. In open institutions the population should be as small as possible.

(4) On the other hand, it is undesirable to maintain prisons which are so small that proper facilities cannot be provided.

64. The duty of society does not end with a prisoner's release. There should, therefore, be governmental or private agencies capable of lending the released prisoner efficient after-care directed towards the lessening of prejudice against him and towards his social rehabilitation.

Treatment

65. The treatment of persons sentenced to imprisonment or a similar measure shall have as its purpose, so far as the length of the sentence permits, to establish in them the will to lead law-abiding and self-supporting lives after their release and to fit them to do so. The treatment shall be such as will encourage their self-respect and develop their sense of responsibility.

66. (1) To these ends, all appropriate means shall be used, including religious care in the countries where this is possible, education, vocational guidance and training, social casework, employment counselling, physical development and strengthening of moral character, in accordance with the individual needs of each prisoner, taking account of his social and criminal history, his physical and mental capacities and aptitudes, his personal temperament, the length of his sentence and his prospects after release.

(2) For every prisoner with a sentence of suitable length, the director shall receive, as soon as possible after his admission, full reports on all the matters referred to in the foregoing paragraph. Such reports shall always include a report by a medical officer, wherever possible qualified in psychiatry, on the physical and mental condition of the prisoner.

(3) The reports and other relevant documents shall be placed in an individual file. This file shall be kept up to date and classified in such a way that it can be consulted by the responsible personnel whenever the need arises.

Classification and individualization

67. The purposes of classification shall be:

(*a*) To separate from others those prisoners who, by reason of their criminal records or bad characters, are likely to exercise a bad influence;

(*b*) To divide the prisoners into classes in order to facilitate their treatment with a view to their social rehabilitation.

68. So far as possible separate institutions or separate sections of an institution shall be used for the treatment of the different classes of prisoners.

69. As soon as possible after admission and after a study of the personality of each prisoner with a sentence of suitable length, a programme of treatment shall be prepared for him in the light of the knowledge obtained about his individual needs, his capacities and dispositions.

Privileges

70. Systems of privileges appropriate for the different classes of prisoners and the different methods of treatment shall be established at every institution, in order to encourage good conduct, develop a sense of responsibility and secure the interest and co-operation of the prisoners in their treatment.

Work

71. (1) Prison labour must not be of an afflictive nature.

(2) All prisoners under sentence shall be required to work, subject to their physical and mental fitness as determined by the medical officer.

(3) Sufficient work of a useful nature shall be provided to keep prisoners actively employed for a normal working day.

(4) So far as possible the work provided shall be such as will maintain or increase the prisoners' ability to earn an honest living after release.

(5) Vocational training in useful trades shall be provided for prisoners able to profit thereby and especially for young prisoners.

(6) Within the limits compatible with proper vocational selection and with the requirements of institutional administration and discipline, the prisoners shall be able to choose the type of work they wish to perform.

72. (1) The organization and methods of work in the institutions shall resemble as closely as possible those of similar work outside institutions, so as to prepare prisoners for the conditions of normal occupational life.

(2) The interests of the prisoners and of their vocational training, however, must not be subordinated to the purpose of making a financial profit from an industry in the institution.

73. (1) Preferably institutional industries and farms should be operated directly by the administration and not by private contractors.

(2) Where prisoners are employed in work not controlled by the administration, they shall always be under the supervision of the institution's personnel. Unless the work is for other departments of the government the full normal wages for such work shall be paid to the administration by the persons to whom the labour is supplied, account being taken of the output of the prisoners.

74. (1) The precautions laid down to protect the safety and health of free workmen shall be equally observed in institutions.

(2) Provision shall be made to indemnify prisoners against industrial injury, including occupational disease, on terms not less favourable than those extended by law to free workmen.

75. (1) The maximum daily and weekly working hours of the prisoners shall be fixed by law or by administrative regulation, taking into account local rules or custom in regard to the employment of free workmen.

(2) The hours so fixed shall leave one rest day a week and sufficient time for education and other activities required as part of the treatment and rehabilitation of the prisoners.

76. (1) There shall be a system of equitable remuneration of the work of prisoners.

(2) Under the system prisoners shall be allowed to spend at least a part of their earnings on approved articles for their own use and to send a part of their earnings to their family.

(3) The system should also provide that a part of the earnings should be set aside by the administration so as to constitute a savings fund to be handed over to the prisoner on his release.

Education and recreation

77. (1) Provision shall be made for the further education of all prisoners capable of profiting thereby, including religious instruction in the countries where this is possible. The education of illiterates and young prisoners shall be compulsory and special attention shall be paid to it by the administration.

(2) So far as practicable, the education of prisoners shall be integrated with the educational system of the country so that after their release they may continue their education without difficulty.

78. Recreational and cultural activities shall be provided in all institutions for the benefit of the mental and physical health of prisoners.

Social relations and after-care

79.   Special attention shall be paid to the maintenance and improvement of such relations between a prisoner and his family as are desirable in the best interests of both.

80.   From the beginning of a prisoner's sentence consideration shall be given to his future after release and he shall be encouraged and assisted to maintain or establish such relations with persons or agencies outside the institution as may promote the best interests of his family and his own social rehabilitation.

81.   (1) Services and agencies, governmental or otherwise, which assist released prisoners to re-establish themselves in society shall ensure, so far as is possible and necessary, that released prisoners be provided with appropriate documents and identification papers, have suitable homes and work to go to, are suitably and adequately clothed having regard to the climate and season, and have sufficient means to reach their destination and maintain themselves in the period immediately following their release.

(2) The approved representatives of such agencies shall have all necessary access to the institution and to prisoners and shall be taken into consultation as to the future of a prisoner from the beginning of his sentence.

(3) It is desirable that the activities of such agencies shall be centralized or co-ordinated as far as possible in order to secure the best use of their efforts.

B. Insane and mentally abnormal prisoners

82.   (1) Persons who are found to be insane shall not be detained in prisons and arrangements shall be made to remove them to mental institutions as soon as possible.

(2) Prisoners who suffer from other mental diseases or abnormalities shall be observed and treated in specialized institutions under medical management.

(3) During their stay in a prison, such prisoners shall be placed under the special supervision of a medical officer.

(4) The medical or psychiatric service of the penal institutions shall provide for the psychiatric treatment of all other prisoners who are in need of such treatment.

83.   It is desirable that steps should be taken, by arrangement with the appropriate agencies, to ensure if necessary the continuation of psychiatric treatment after release and the provision of social-psychiatric after-care.

C. Prisoners under arrest or awaiting trial

84.   (1) Persons arrested or imprisoned by reason of a criminal charge against them, who are detained either in police custody or in prison custody

(jail) but have not yet been tried and sentenced, will be referred to as "untried prisoners" hereinafter in these rules.

(2) Unconvicted prisoners are presumed to be innocent and shall be treated as such.

(3) Without prejudice to legal rules for the protection of individual liberty or prescribing the procedure to be observed in respect of untried prisoners, these prisoners shall benefit by a special régime which is described in the following rules in its essential requirements only.

85. (1) Untried prisoners shall be kept separate from convicted prisoners.

(2) Young untried prisoners shall be kept separate from adults and shall in principle be detained in separate institutions.

86. Untried prisoners shall sleep singly in separate rooms, with the reservation of different local custom in respect of the climate.

87. Within the limits compatible with the good order of the institution, untried prisoners may, if they so desire, have their food procured at their own expense from the outside, either through the administration or through their family or friends. Otherwise, the administration shall provide their food.

88. (1) An untried prisoner shall be allowed to wear his own clothing if it is clean and suitable.

(2) If he wears prison dress, it shall be different from that supplied to convicted prisoners.

89. An untried prisoner shall always be offered opportunity to work, but shall not be required to work. If he chooses to work, he shall be paid for it.

90. An untried prisoner shall be allowed to procure at his own expense or at the expense of a third party such books, newspapers, writing materials and other means of occupation as are compatible with the interests of the administration of justice and the security and good order of the institution.

91. An untried prisoner shall be allowed to be visited and treated by his own doctor or dentist if there is reasonable ground for his application and he is able to pay any expenses incurred.

92. An untried prisoner shall be allowed to inform immediately his family of his detention and shall be given all reasonable facilities for communicating with his family and friends, and for receiving visits from them, subject only to restrictions and supervision as are necessary in the interests of the administration of justice and of the security and good order of the institution.

93. For the purposes of his defence, an untried prisoner shall be allowed to apply for free legal aid where such aid is available, and to receive visits from his legal adviser with a view to his defence and to prepare and hand to him

confidential instructions. For these purposes, he shall if he so desires be supplied with writing material. Interviews between the prisoner and his legal adviser may be within sight but not within the hearing of a police or institution official.

D. CIVIL PRISONERS

94.   In countries where the law permits imprisonment for debt, or by order of a court under any other non-criminal process, persons so imprisoned shall not be subjected to any greater restriction or severity than is necessary to ensure safe custody and good order. Their treatment shall be not less favourable than that of untried prisoners, with the reservation, however, that they may possibly be required to work.

E. PERSONS ARRESTED OR DETAINED WITHOUT CHARGE

95.   Without prejudice to the provisions of article 9 of the International Covenant on Civil and Political Rights, persons arrested or imprisoned without charge shall be accorded the same protection as that accorded under part I and part II, section C. Relevant provisions of part II, section A, shall likewise be applicable where their application may be conducive to the benefit of this special group of persons in custody, provided that no measures shall be taken implying that re-education or rehabilitation is in any way appropriate to persons not convicted of any criminal offence.

Freedom of Association and Protection of the Right to Organise Convention

CONVENTION (No. 87) CONCERNING FREEDOM OF ASSOCIATION
AND PROTECTION OF THE RIGHT TO ORGANISE

*Adopted on 9 July 1948 by the General Conference of the International Labour
Organisation at its thirty-first session*

ENTRY INTO FORCE: 4 July 1950. in accordance with article 15

The General Conference of the International Labour Organisation,

Having been convened at San Francisco by the Governing Body of the
International Labour Office, and having met in its thirty-first session on 17
June 1948,

Having decided to adopt, in the form of a Convention, certain proposals
concerning freedom of association and protection of the right to organise
which is the seventh item on the agenda of the session,

Considering that the Preamble to the Constitution of the International
Labour Organisation declares "recognition of the principle of freedom of
association" to be a means of improving conditions of labour and of establishing peace,

Considering that the Declaration of Philadelphia reaffirms that "freedom
of expression and of association are essential to sustained progress",

Considering that the International Labour Conference, at its thirtieth
session, unanimously adopted the principles which should form the basis for
international regulation,

Considering that the General Assembly of the United Nations, at its
second session, endorsed these principles and requested the International
Labour Organisation to continue every effort in order that it may be possible
to adopt one or several international Conventions,

Adopts this ninth day of July of the year one thousand nine hundred and
forty-eight the following Convention. which may be cited as the Freedom of
Association and Protection of the Right to Organise Convention, 1948:

PART I

FREEDOM OF ASSOCIATION

Article 1

Each Member of the International Labour Organisation for which this Convention is in force undertakes to give effect to the following provisions.

Article 2

Workers and employers, without distinction whatsoever, shall have the right to establish and, subject only to the rules of the organisation concerned, to join organisations of their own choosing without previous authorisation.

Article 3

1.   Workers' and employers' organisations shall have the right to draw up their constitutions and rules, to elect their representatives in full freedom, to organise their administration and activities and to formulate their programmes.

2.   The public authorities shall refrain from any interference which would restrict this right or impede the lawful exercise thereof.

Article 4

Workers' and employers' organisations shall not be liable to be dissolved or suspended by administrative authority.

Article 5

Workers' and employers' organisations shall have the right to establish and join federations and confederations and any such organisation, federation or confederation shall have the right to affiliate with international organisations of workers and employers.

Article 6

The provisions of articles 2, 3 and 4 hereof apply to federations and confederations of workers' and employers' organisations.

Article 7

The acquisition of legal personality by workers' and employers' organisations, federations and confederations shall not be made subject to conditions of such a character as to restrict the application of the provisions of articles 2, 3 and 4 hereof.

Article 8

1. In exercising the rights provided for in this Convention workers and employers and their respective organisations, like other persons or organised collectivities, shall respect the law of the land.

2. The law of the land shall not be such as to impair, nor shall it be so applied as to impair, the guarantees provided for in this Convention.

Article 9

1. The extent to which the guarantees provided for in this Convention shall apply to the armed forces and the police shall be determined by national laws or regulations.

2. In accordance with the principle set forth in paragraph 8 of article 19 of the Constitution of the International Labour Organisation, the ratification of this Convention by any Member shall not be deemed to affect any existing law, award, custom or agreement in virtue of which members of the armed forces or the police enjoy any right guaranteed by this Convention.

Article 10

In this Convention the term "organisation" means any organisation of workers or of employers for furthering and defending the interests of workers or of employers.

PART II

PROTECTION OF THE RIGHT TO ORGANISE

Article 11

Each Member of the International Labour Organisation for which this Convention is in force undertakes to take all necessary and appropriate measures to ensure that workers and employers may exercise freely the right to organise.

PART III

MISCELLANEOUS PROVISIONS

Article 12

1. In respect of the territories referred to in article 35 of the Constitution of the International Labour Organisation as amended by the Constitution of

the International Labour Organisation Instrument of Amendment, 1946, other than the territories referred to in paragraphs 4 and 5 of the said article as so amended, each Member of the Organisation which ratifies this Convention shall communicate to the Director-General of the International Labour Office with or as soon as possible after its ratification a declaration stating:

(*a*) The territories in respect of which it undertakes that the provisions of the Convention shall be applied without modification;

(*b*) The territories in respect of which it undertakes that the provisions of the Convention shall be applied subject to modifications, together with details of the said modifications;

(*c*) The territories in respect of which the Convention is inapplicable and in such cases the grounds on which it is inapplicable;

(*d*) The territories in respect of which it reserves its decision.

2. The undertakings referred to in subparagraphs (*a*) and (*b*) of paragraph 1 of this article shall be deemed to be an integral part of the ratification and shall have the force of ratification.

3. Any Member may at any time by a subsequent declaration cancel in whole or in part any reservations made in its original declaration in virtue of subparagraphs (*b*), (*c*) or (*d*) of paragraph 1 of this article.

4. Any Member may, at any time at which this Convention is subject to denunciation in accordance with the provisions of article 16, communicate to the Director-General a declaration modifying in any other respect the terms of any former declaration and stating the present position in respect of such territories as it may specify.

Article 13

1. Where the subject-matter of this Convention is within the self-governing powers of any non-metropolitan territory, the Member responsible for the international relations of that territory may, in agreement with the government of the territory, communicate to the Director-General of the International Labour Office a declaration accepting on behalf of the territory the obligations of this Convention.

2. A declaration accepting the obligations of this Convention may be communicated to the Director-General of the International Labour Office:

(*a*) By two or more Members of the Organisation in respect of any territory which is under their joint authority; or

(*b*) By any international authority responsible for the administration of any territory, in virtue of the Charter of the United Nations or otherwise, in respect of any such territory.

3. Declarations communicated to the Director-General of the International Labour Office in accordance with the preceding paragraphs of this article shall indicate whether the provisions of the Convention will be applied in the territory concerned without modification or subject to modifications; when the declaration indicates that the provisions of the Convention will be applied subject to modifications it shall give details of the said modifications.

4. The Member, Members or international authority concerned may at any time by a subsequent declaration renounce in whole or in part the right to have recourse to any modification indicated in any former declaration.

5. The Member, Members or international authority concerned may, at any time at which this Convention is subject to denunciation in accordance with the provisions of article 16, communicate to the Director-General of the International Labour Office a declaration modifying in any other respect the terms of any former declaration and stating the present position in respect of the application of the Convention.

PART IV

FINAL PROVISIONS

Article 14

The formal ratifications of this Convention shall be communicated to the Director-General of the International Labour Office for registration.

Article 15

1. This Convention shall be binding only upon those Members of the International Labour Organisation whose ratifications have been registered with the Director-General.

2. It shall come into force twelve months after the date on which the ratifications of two Members have been registered with the Director-General.

3. Thereafter, this Convention shall come into force for any Member twelve months after the date on which its ratification has been registered.

Article 16

1. A Member which has ratified this Convention may denounce it after the expiration of ten years from the date on which the Convention first comes into force, by an act communicated to the Director-General of the International Labour Office for registration. Such denunciation shall not take effect until one year after the date on which it is registered.

2. Each Member which has ratified this Convention and which does not, within the year following the expiration of the period of ten years mentioned in the preceding paragraph, exercise the right of denunciation provided

for in this article, will be bound for another period of ten years and, thereafter, may denounce this Convention at the expiration of each period of ten years under the terms provided for in this article.

Article 17

1.   The Director-General of the International Labour Office shall notify all Members of the International Labour Organisation of the registration of all ratifications, declarations and denunciations communicated to him by the Members of the Organisation.

2.   When notifying the Members of the Organisation of the registration of the second ratification communicated to him, the Director-General shall draw the attention of the Members of the Organisation to the date upon which the Convention will come into force.

Article 18

The Director-General of the International Labour Office shall communicate to the Secretary-General of the United Nations for registration in accordance with Article 102 of the Charter of the United Nations full particulars of all ratifications, declarations and acts of denunciation registered by him in accordance with the provisions of the preceding articles.

Article 19

At the expiration of each period of ten years after the coming into force of this Convention, the Governing Body of the International Labour Office shall present to the General Conference a report on the working of this Convention and shall consider the desirability of placing on the agenda of the Conference the question of its revision in whole or in part.

Article 20

1.   Should the Conference adopt a new Convention revising this Convention in whole or in part, then, unless the new Convention otherwise provides:

(a) The ratification by a Member of the new revising Convention shall *ipso jure* involve the immediate denunciation of this Convention, notwithstanding the provisions of article 16 above, if and when the new revising Convention shall have come into force;

(b) As from the date when the new revising Convention comes into force this Convention shall cease to be open to ratification by the Members.

2.   This Convention shall in any case remain in force in its actual form and content for those Members which have ratified it but have not ratified the revising Convention.

Article 21

The English and French versions of the text of this Convention are equally authoritative.

The foregoing is the authentic text of the Convention duly adopted by the General Conference of the International Labour Organisation during its thirty-first session which was held at San Francisco and declared closed the tenth day of July 1948.

IN FAITH WHEREOF we have appended our signatures this thirty-first day of August 1948.

Declaration of the Rights of the Child

Proclaimed by General Assembly resolution 1386 (XIV) of 20 November 1959

PREAMBLE

Whereas the peoples of the United Nations have, in the Charter, re-affirmed their faith in fundamental human rights and in the dignity and worth of the human person, and have determined to promote social progress and better standards of life in larger freedom,

Whereas the United Nations has, in the Universal Declaration of Human Rights, proclaimed that everyone is entitled to all the rights and freedoms set forth therein, without distinction of any kind, such as race, colour, sex, language, religion, political or other opinion, national or social origin, property, birth or other status,

Whereas the child, by reason of his physical and mental immaturity, needs special safeguards and care, including appropriate legal protection, before as well as after birth,

Whereas the need for such special safeguards has been stated in the Geneva Declaration of the Rights of the Child of 1924, and recognized in the Universal Declaration of Human Rights and in the statutes of specialized agencies and international organizations concerned with the welfare of children,

Whereas mankind owes to the child the best it has to give,

Now therefore,

The General Assembly

Proclaims this Declaration of the Rights of the Child to the end that he may have a happy childhood and enjoy for his own good and for the good of society the rights and freedoms herein set forth, and calls upon parents, upon men and women as individuals, and upon voluntary organizations, local authorities and national Governments to recognize these rights and strive for their observance by legislative and other measures progressively taken in accordance with the following principles:

Principle 1

The child shall enjoy all the rights set forth in this Declaration. Every child, without any exception whatsoever, shall be entitled to these rights, without distinction or discrimination on account of race, colour, sex, language, religion, political or other opinion, national or social origin, property, birth or other status, whether of himself or of his family.

Principle 2

The child shall enjoy special protection, and shall be given opportunities and facilities, by law and by other means, to enable him to develop physically, mentally, morally, spiritually and socially in a healthy and normal manner and in conditions of freedom and dignity. In the enactment of laws for this purpose, the best interests of the child shall be the paramount consideration.

Principle 3

The child shall be entitled from his birth to a name and a nationality.

Principle 4

The child shall enjoy the benefits of social security. He shall be entitled to grow and develop in health; to this end, special care and protection shall be provided both to him and to his mother, including adequate pre-natal and post-natal care. The child shall have the right to adequate nutrition, housing, recreation and medical services.

Principle 5

The child who is physically, mentally or socially handicapped shall be given the special treatment, education and care required by his particular condition.

Principle 6

The child, for the full and harmonious development of his personality, needs love and understanding. He shall, wherever possible, grow up in the care and under the responsibility of his parents, and, in any case, in an atmosphere of affection and of moral and material security; a child of tender years shall not, save in exceptional circumstances, be separated from his mother. Society and the public authorities shall have the duty to extend particular care to children without a family and to those without adequate means of support. Payment of State and other assistance towards the maintenance of children of large families is desirable.

Principle 7

The child is entitled to receive education, which shall be free and compulsory, at least in the elementary stages. He shall be given an education which will promote his general culture and enable him, on a basis of equal opportunity, to develop his abilities, his individual judgement, and his sense of moral and social responsibility, and to become a useful member of society.

The best interests of the child shall be the guiding principle of those responsible for his education and guidance; that responsibility lies in the first place with his parents.

The child shall have full opportunity for play and recreation, which should be directed to the same purposes as education; society and the public authorities shall endeavour to promote the enjoyment of this right.

Principle 8

The child shall in all circumstances be among the first to receive protection and relief.

Principle 9

The child shall be protected against all forms of neglect, cruelty and exploitation. He shall not be the subject of traffic, in any form.

The child shall not be admitted to employment before an appropriate minimum age; he shall in no case be caused or permitted to engage in any occupation or employment which would prejudice his health or education, or interfere with his physical, mental or moral development.

Principle 10

The child shall be protected from practices which may foster racial, religious and any other form of discrimination. He shall be brought up in a spirit of understanding, tolerance, friendship among peoples, peace and universal brotherhood, and in full consciousness that his energy and talents should be devoted to the service of his fellow men.

Declaration on the Rights of Mentally Retarded Persons

Proclaimed by General Assembly resolution 2856 (XXVI) of 20 December 1971

The General Assembly,

Mindful of the pledge of the States Members of the United Nations under the Charter to take joint and separate action in co-operation with the Organization to promote higher standards of living, full employment and conditions of economic and social progress and development,

Reaffirming faith in human rights and fundamental freedoms and in the principles of peace, of the dignity and worth of the human person and of social justice proclaimed in the Charter,

Recalling the principles of the Universal Declaration of Human Rights, the International Covenants on Human Rights, the Declaration of the Rights of the Child and the standards already set for social progress in the constitutions, conventions, recommendations and resolutions of the International Labour Organisation, the United Nations Educational, Scientific and Cultural Organization, the World Health Organization, the United Nations Children's Fund and other organizations concerned,

Emphasizing that the Declaration on Social Progress and Development has proclaimed the necessity of protecting the rights and assuring the welfare and rehabilitation of the physically and mentally disadvantaged,

Bearing in mind the necessity of assisting mentally retarded persons to develop their abilities in various fields of activities and of promoting their integration as far as possible in normal life,

Aware that certain countries, at their present stage of development, can devote only limited efforts to this end,

Proclaims this Declaration on the Rights of Mentally Retarded Persons and calls for national and international action to ensure that it will be used as a common basis and frame of reference for the protection of these rights:

1.   The mentally retarded person has, to the maximum degree of feasibility, the same rights as other human beings.

2.   The mentally retarded person has a right to proper medical care and physical therapy and to such education, training, rehabilitation and guidance as will enable him to develop his ability and maximum potential.

3.   The mentally retarded person has a right to economic security and to a decent standard of living. He has a right to perform productive work or to engage in any other meaningful occupation to the fullest possible extent of his capabilities.

4.   Whenever possible, the mentally retarded person should live with his own family or with foster parents and participate in different forms of community life. The family with which he lives should receive assistance. If care in an institution becomes necessary, it should be provided in surroundings and other circumstances as close as possible to those of normal life.

5.   The mentally retarded person has a right to a qualified guardian when this is required to protect his personal well-being and interests.

6.   The mentally retarded person has a right to protection from exploitation, abuse and degrading treatment. If prosecuted for any offence, he shall have a right to due process of law with full recognition being given to his degree of mental responsibility.

7.   Whenever mentally retarded persons are unable, because of the severity of their handicap, to exercise all their rights in a meaningful way or it should become necessary to restrict or deny some or all of these rights, the procedure used for that restriction or denial of rights must contain proper legal safeguards against every form of abuse. This procedure must be based on an evaluation of the social capability of the mentally retarded person by qualified experts and must be subject to periodic review and to the right of appeal to higher authorities.

Declaration on the Rights
of Disabled Persons

Proclaimed by General Assembly resolution 3447 (XXX) of 9 December 1975

The General Assembly,

Mindful of the pledge made by Member States, under the Charter of the United Nations to take joint and separate action in co-operation with the Organization to promote higher standards of living, full employment and conditions of economic and social progress and development,

Reaffirming its faith in human rights and fundamental freedoms and in the principles of peace, of the dignity and worth of the human person and of social justice proclaimed in the Charter,

Recalling the principles of the Universal Declaration of Human Rights, the International Covenants on Human Rights, the Declaration of the Rights of the Child and the Declaration on the Rights of Mentally Retarded Persons, as well as the standards already set for social progress in the constitutions, conventions, recommendations and resolutions of the International Labour Organisation, the United Nations Educational, Scientific and Cultural Organization, the World Health Organization, the United Nations Children's Fund and other organizations concerned,

Recalling also Economic and Social Council resolution 1921 (LVIII) of 6 May 1975 on the prevention of disability and the rehabilitation of disabled persons,

Emphasizing that the Declaration on Social Progress and Development has proclaimed the necessity of protecting the rights and assuring the welfare and rehabilitation of the physically and mentally disadvantaged,

Bearing in mind the necessity of preventing physical and mental disabilities and of assisting disabled persons to develop their abilities in the most varied fields of activities and of promoting their integration as far as possible in normal life,

Aware that certain countries, at their present stage of development, can devote only limited efforts to this end,

Proclaims this Declaration on the Rights of Disabled Persons and calls for national and international action to ensure that it will be used as a common basis and frame of reference for the protection of these rights:

1.   The term "disabled person" means any person unable to ensure by himself or herself, wholly or partly, the necessities of a normal individual

and/or social life, as a result of deficiency, either congenital or not, in his or her physical or mental capabilities.

2. Disabled persons shall enjoy all the rights set forth in this Declaration. These rights shall be granted to all disabled persons without any exception whatsoever and without distinction or discrimination on the basis of race, colour, sex, language, religion, political or other opinions, national or social origin, state of wealth, birth or any other situation applying either to the disabled person himself or herself or to his or her family.

3. Disabled persons have the inherent right to respect for their human dignity. Disabled persons, whatever the origin, nature and seriousness of their handicaps and disabilities, have the same fundamental rights as their fellow-citizens of the same age, which implies first and foremost the right to enjoy a decent life, as normal and full as possible.

4. Disabled persons have the same civil and political rights as other human beings; paragraph 7 of the Declaration on the Rights of Mentally Retarded Persons applies to any possible limitation or suppression of those rights for mentally disabled persons.

5. Disabled persons are entitled to the measures designed to enable them to become as self-reliant as possible.

6. Disabled persons have the right to medical, psychological and functional treatment, including prosthetic and orthetic appliances, to medical and social rehabilitation, education, vocational training and rehabilitation, aid, counselling, placement services and other services which will enable them to develop their capabilities and skills to the maximum and will hasten the processes of their social integration or reintegration.

7. Disabled persons have the right to economic and social security and to a decent level of living. They have the right, according to their capabilities, to secure and retain employment or to engage in a useful, productive and remunerative occupation and to join trade unions.

8. Disabled persons are entitled to have their special needs taken into consideration at all stages of economic and social planning.

9. Disabled persons have the right to live with their families or with foster parents and to participate in all social, creative or recreational activities. No disabled person shall be subjected, as far as his or her residence is concerned, to differential treatment other than that required by his or her condition or by the improvement which he or she may derive therefrom. If the stay of a disabled person in a specialized establishment is indispensable, the environment and living conditions therein shall be as close as possible to those of the normal life of a person of his or her age.

10. Disabled persons shall be protected against all exploitation, all regulations and all treatment of a discriminatory, abusive or degrading nature.

11.   Disabled persons shall be able to avail themselves of qualified legal aid when such aid proves indispensable for the protection of their persons and property. If judicial proceedings are instituted against them, the legal procedure applied shall take their physical and mental condition fully into account.

12.   Organizations of disabled persons may be usefully consulted in all matters regarding the rights of disabled persons.

13.   Disabled persons, their families and communities shall be fully informed, by all appropriate means, of the rights contained in this Declaration.

Index

Human Rights Commission, 3,
26, 55–56, 93
publications, 67, 93–94, 97
Sub-Committee on the Prevention
of Discrimination and Protec-
tion of Minorities, 55
Working Group on Enforced and
Involuntary "Disappearances,"
4, 55
See also International Labour
Organisation; Universal Decla-
ration of Human Rights; spe-
cific conventions
*U.N. Action in the Field of Human
Rights,* 94
*The U.N. Commission on Human
Rights,* 93
U.N. Educational, Scientific, and
Cultural Organization. *See*
UNESCO
United States
human rights record of, 5–6,
115–116
legal system of, 82, 97–98
See also U.S. foreign policy
U.S. Catholic Mission Association,
49
U.S. Committee on Foreign Affairs,
66
U.S. Department of Human Rights
and Humanitarian Affairs, 6
U.S. Department of State, 56, 83,
94
U.S. foreign policy, 79, 83, 94
and Argentina, 29
Carter Administration approach
to, 6, 16, 20–21
and Latin America, 45, 48, 68, 69
and Liberia, 75
watchdog organizations, 40, 41,
42, 47
Universal Declaration of Human
Rights, 1, 2–3, 115, 117–122
employment rights, 6
freedom of expression, 43
and Jewish law, 77
organizations promoting, 35
Palestinian rights, 53
publications on, 75–76, 84, 85,
93–94, 100

racial discrimination, 13
Universal Declaration on the Eradi-
cation of Hunger and Malnutri-
tion, 15
Universal Islamic Declaration of
Human Rights, 18
University of the Philippines Col-
lege and Center for Law, 90
Untouchability, 108
Urban areas, human rights in, 93
Urban Morgan Institute for Human
Rights, 100
U.S.S.R. *See* Soviet Union

Van Dijk, P., 75
Van Dyke, Vernon, 94
Van Niekerk, Barend, 94–95
Veatch, Henry B., 95
Verstappen, Berth, 95
Vincent, R. J., 95
*Violations of Human Rights: Possible
Rights of Recourse and Forms of
Resistance,* 93
Voices for Freedom, 74
Voices of the Voiceless, 108
Voyage of Dreams, 108–109

Walesa, Lech, 31
*The War against Children: South
Africa's Youngest Victims,* 86
War crimes, 14
War victims, 11, 15
Welch, Claude E., 95–96
Western Europe, 62
Wiesel, Elie, 32
Wiesenthal, Simon, 32–33
Wilsonline, 112–113
*WIN (Women's International Network)
News,* 101–102
Wiseberg, Laurie S., 62–63, 90
*With Friends Like These: The Americas
Watch Report on Human Rights and
U.S. Policy in Latin America,* 68
*Without Justice for All: The Constitu-
tional Rights of Aliens,* 82
Wombat Film and Video, 111
Women, 14, 15, 16, 17, 18, 101–102
under apartheid, 106
and marriage, 12
sexual exploitation of, 109–110